To Todd.

I hope this book brings

You even closer to

your father.

Omari Daniel

4-21-04.

You can truly
Leave no child
Behind with your
work
Jack Daniel

WE FISH

WE FiSH

THE JOURNEY
TO FATHERHOOD

Jack L. Daniel & Omari C. Daniel

UNIVERSITY OF PITTSBURGH PRESS

Published by the University of Pittsburgh Press, Pittsburgh, Pa., 15260
Copyright © 2003, University of Pittsburgh Press
All rights reserved
Manufactured in the United States of America
Printed on acid-free paper
10 9 8 7 6 5 4 3 2 1
ISBN 0-8229-4198-8

CONTENTS

ACKNOWLEDGMENTS

We dedicate this work of hope to the African American male generation of Javon Tyson Daniel, the youngest "Daniel Man," who was born on May 9, 2001. Let him, his children, and his children's children always contribute to the well being of others.

With this writing, we seek to nurture the spirits of Russell P. Daniel Sr., Manuel Daniel Sr., Nash Young, and William Young. All were living examples of determination in the face of improbable odds, creativity when constantly confronted by necessity, generosity notwithstanding limited material resources, and African American fatherhood forged in the crucible of American racism.

Uncles Nash and William showed us the ways of fishermen, and provided us with the special outdoor opportunity to bond with them as well as with Bryan S. Daniel, Robert Daniel Lavelle, David Young, Stephen B. Daniel, and Henry Harris—a bonding we believe to be instructive for other African American men. We are especially appreciative of Robert Daniel Lavelle's parents, Bob and Phillis, who permitted their son to join our circle, thus allowing him to become more than a nephew and a cousin for us.

From conception to completion, Mark A. Nordenberg, Lee Gutkind, and William Isler believed in our creative capacities and remained encouraging. This work was also made possible by James V. Maher's support of Jack L. Daniel making creative uses of his summers.

We are especially appreciative of the sustenance that we received from the following key women: Our mother and grandmother Grace C. Daniel's spirit dwells deep within us and nearly all that she touched; Aunt Minnie Daniel was the truest form of an "other mother," a mother for Jack during those summers he spent at her home; Professor Toi Dericotte at the University of Pittsburgh, as well as through Cave Canem, helped shape the original "We Fish" poems; Patricia Parks provided essential and timely editorial assistance; Dr. Marijata Daniel Echols provided a "womanist" critique; Cherice Tyson Daniel shared her home as a writing refuge; and Jerlean Evelyn Colley Daniel mothered Omari and nurtured both of us through our evolving senses of manhood. We also thank her for the many times that she read this manuscript and used her "developmentalist" approach to provide critical feedback throughout the writing process.

Knowing that the future of African American men is inextricably bound to African American women, we also dedicate this work to two strong African American women in the making, i.e., Amani Danielle Echols and Akili Colley Echols. In doing so, we also take note of the extraordinary example of African American fatherhood being provided for them by Anthony Wellington Echols, a strong sign of hope for African American fathers to come.

WE FISH

PROLOGUE

I FELT a strange, confusing pain when, during a 1993 Kwanzaa celebration, I heard a sixteen-year-old African American male give thanks for
having lived to see his sixteenth birthday.

I read the January first front-page news stories detailing county mur-
der victims for 1993 and 1994; most of them were African Americans.

From 1980 to 1993, young African American males had a 63 percent
increase in suicides.

I longed for solutions rather than yet another recitation of statistics
associated with young black men killing each other, themselves, and
others, day after day. One woman, quoted in the newspaper noted, in-
sightfully, I thought: "We don't need any more forecasts of rain. We need
to build the ark."

I was stuck in a slow funk of depression. I'd had a lot to say about all
aspects of African American life as a black revolutionary college student in
the 1960s, but now had so little to say about resolving African Americans'
problems in the 1990s. In the midst of these thoughts, my son, Omari,
shared with me some poems he had written. As I read them, I experienced a surge of excitement: this young man had escaped the time period

and circumstances that had caused others to be jailed, killed, or in other ways destroyed. My son was in college, and had made the Dean's List. It was *my son* who was expressing profound thoughts about life.

Omari had written about the deepening of our father and son relationship while we were fishing. At first, as far as Omari's poems about fishing were concerned, I just didn't get it. Omari and I had always fished together; I had never seen our fishing together as anything other than, well, just fishing. I loved fishing so much that I had been nicknamed the Bassman. For years, I thought I had only been sharing my love of fishing with my son, my father, and other important men in my life. However, the content of Omari's poems made me see a connection between the time we had spent fishing and the relationships we had built with each other and the other men in our family. Reading these poems, I was reminded that at least four consecutive generations of "Daniel men" had more than survived, despite the mountains and valleys each had needed to conquer. His poems shed light on the strengths of the men in his life who had helped him grow—and on the way that fishing had given us a space within which to share those strengths and that growing process. Reading Omari's work, I began thinking about the substance necessary for the building of that ark.

A rush of ideas came to me, and I wanted to express them. Omari would write poems, and I would write related essays. Maybe something real and meaningful could be said about African American male development outside the confines of sociopolitical texts. Maybe, from our fishing experiences, we could glean some answers to some of the problems facing African American males in structural poverty. And maybe my time in the struggle had not passed; maybe I did have something to say about building the ark. At about the same time I was experiencing this excitement of ideas, came a tremendous Father's Day gift.

Reflections On Father's Day

Daddy, you've written us so many letters like this over the years, I figured it was about time to write you one in return. When I think about many of my friends, and the many young black people in this country who have never had any reason to celebrate a Father's Day, it really makes me think about how lucky I am. As a Daniel Man you were only doing what was expected, or par for the course, so I can't give you too much credit for that, but I am lucky to have a father who took the time to do so many things with me.

When I beat people in cards, they ask me how I did it, and I tell them I learned to play cards sitting on my father's knee when I was in second and third grade. The same thing happens in ping-pong, and just about any other game that I play. It is not so much the actual play of the game, but general strategies that I picked up, and employ in my everyday activities, be it playing to win, finessing, engaging in psychological warfare, or occasionally bending the rules. (I know you are probably sitting there acting like you don't do these things, but you do, and I do, and we both win all the time.)

The things you did with me and for me, as you know, go far beyond games. Basically, as I have expressed in some poems, you made me into a Daniel Man, and you know—all of the things like loving yourself, taking care of your family, etc., that go along with that. It's funny, but a lot of things it seemed like you were *doing to me* at that time, were really being *done for me*. A perfect example of this is when I am editing other people's papers, or my own for that matter, and I have to put in commas. Every time that I add missing commas, I think back to when you would leave me sentences to do when I came home from school, and I smile or chuckle to myself. Well, I guess I'll move on. I wouldn't want to gas your head up too much. After all, we have your age and blood pressure to worry about (Ha, Ha).

I have been thinking about your book idea. The more I think about it, and the more I see going wrong with black men in this country, the more I think the book might be a necessity. We need to discuss the idea more, and lay out the project, because I would hate to miss this opportunity. We at least owe it to ourselves to look into the book idea a little more to see if it is possible.

I think I only have one more topic for this letter, and that is fishing. Over the years, I have never quite had the fever for fishing like you have, and I suppose that is what keeps you on top. But I love going, and wouldn't trade the time I spend fishing with you for anything. When I hear stories of you going with other people, I get a little jealous, but then I am happy that you got to enjoy yourself. When you go by yourself, I wish I were there. I am glad when you catch fish, and love the sound of your voice, and the excitement in it when you tell the stories, and I kind of feel like I was there. I don't really like fishing with other people but so much. It is fun. I spend most of the time playing or talking stuff with the friend I am with, but it isn't really fishing. It is only "fishing" when you are there, because it is "us" together, and I cherish those moments more than you can imagine. Thanks!

Omari,
Bassman Jr.

It took a day for me to collect my emotions before I could talk about this with Omari. The next evening, I called him, thanked him for the letter and proposed that we begin this book, focusing on his earliest childhood memories of our fishing. He was emphatic in his response. "No, Daddy. You need to begin by figuring out why you have the 'fever' when it comes to fishing."

I was so overjoyed at the prospect of writing with my son that I agreed, even though, at that time, I didn't know exactly what the "fever" meant. Nor was I anywhere near understanding how my "fever" might have anything to do with helping to build the ark African American men needed so desperately. I only know that its force propelled me forward.

Thus, the journey began.

2

COULDN'T SEE FOR LOOKING

THE FACT that my son Omari was writing at all, let alone poetry, came as a surprise. He had to be force-fed his handwriting assignments in grade school. His poor penmanship, in my mind, was a reflection of the carelessness that he exhibited with his academic work. As time went on, I found myself having to constantly remind him of the importance of doing well academically and that his school work must come before recreation.

I had always emphasized to my children the importance of learning well at least three "alphabets." I told Omari and my daughter, Marijata, that if they could master A through Z, 0 through 9, and a third alphabet, then they would not only do well at school, but also at whatever else they wished to do in life. The third alphabet could be sharps and flats, the primary colors, dance steps, or any other set of artistic symbols. Ours is a society reliant upon symbols, and I believed that if they mastered the two key alphabets, along with an artistic one, then racism and sexism would have a hard time holding them back. Whether Marijata understood and applied this formula consciously, or whether she was simply self-motivated,

she excelled consistently in all areas. But with Omari, I had to continu-
ally hammer home the basic lessons because of what seemed to me to be
his desire to avoid working at the highest level of his academic potential.
On paper, he misspelled words that I knew he could spell correctly; he'd
get the right answers to his arithmetic problems, but only do part of what
was required in the assignment. At one point during his elementary years,
I almost gave up entirely on his acquisition of a third alphabet, because
it was so difficult to get him to master the two basic ones.

When Omari was in first grade, my wife Jerri and I moved to a suburban town where she was the director of a child care center; she loved
her job, and the twenty mile commute from the city, coupled with the
difficulty of finding quality child care, had become a hassle. We wanted
our children to have the opportunity to interact with other children of
color while living in this predominantly white, upper class community,
so we enrolled them in the public school system rather than the local
private academy. We certainly did not want them to have an additional
opportunity to develop elitist attitudes.

Throughout first and second grade, ongoing battles took place between Omari and his teachers and parents. We adults were convinced of
his academic potential, but Omari seemed determined to extend the play-
ground to the classroom. Periodically, Jerri or I (or both of us) visited with
his teachers and heard about his taunting and teasing of his peers, with
some incidents culminating in fistfights. The largest second grade incident included the allegation that, at recess time, Omari caught a spider
in a plastic bag, later released it in his classroom, and caused a near stam-
pede of children running out of the room when he announced, "Look, a
black widow spider."

In third grade, Omari had a black teacher who took a no-nonsense
approach with him and insisted that he excel. That year he did extremely
well and subsequently finished grade school without dropping below a B
average. This still wasn't good enough for my black male child. My father had been rejected by West Point, supposedly because he had failed
the admission exam by one point; Jerri's father was denied admission to

the University of Alabama Law School, allegedly for academic reasons, although he later was admitted to Yale Law. Accordingly, I viewed Omari's B average as a baseline for improvement in junior high school; anything less than an A had the potential for being a racially motivated act against him. I had to stay on him, ride him, guide him.

Junior and early senior high school English writing classes continued to be traumatic experiences for Omari and his teachers. For the first quarter in ninth grade, Omari received all B grades and one A. Trying to be supportive of Omari, but also to remind him that more was expected of him, and as an alert to his teachers, I wrote on the back of his report card, "We are pleased with Omari's first quarter's performance. Omari has set a goal of improving in everything. We have agreed with his goal. Please let us know, as time passes, if he is improving, and how we can help him improve. Halfway through the second quarter, if he is not improving, please call me for a conference. Thanks."

My written message was extremely important to me because of the low academic expectations that many teachers have for African American males. Additionally, these children all too often have low expectations for themselves, having received no encouragement from any other arena. Educators had documented the significant lag that occurred by third grade for black children as compared to whites. In many public schools, the predominantly white teachers' expectations were so low that a B grade was deemed wonderful for an African American male; I called it the "B for a black boy" syndrome. I was not going to have either Omari or his teachers believing that B was a satisfactorily high level of academic achievement for my son. I knew that Omari could well face racial discrimination in college and later, in the work world, even if he was fully qualified academically. I worried endlessly about what would happen to him if his grades were less than outstanding. His seemingly conscious lack of effort appeared to be heading him in all of the wrong directions.

During the ninth grade, Omari was showing great promise in several track events, but I was determined to not let him go down what I considered to be a socially preordained athletic road. Maybe he and his teachers thought that his first quarter report card with all Bs and one A was something wonderful, but I had to let them know that "good" wasn't "good enough" for Omari. I read to him my written comments to make sure that he knew he needed to convert some of those Bs into As, particularly in English and math. Jerri, too, gave reinforcement with one of her "bedtime talks."

When Omari had been in elementary school, Jerri and I had watched in dismay as, throughout Pittsburgh, many of the African American boys were tracked into peewee running backs, fifty-meter sprinters, little league catchers, and young jump shooters. We watched later as, one by one, many of these same kids experienced difficulties in specific academic areas, failed grades, and got placed on the athletic "fast track." Observing this pattern, and having noted the same thing with many of our own friends when we attended public schools years ago, Jerri and I made academic success a prerequisite for Omari to engage in athletic competition. It seemed that he had really understood our messages when one of Omari's coaches tried to convince him that athletics should play a greater role in his life, and that he should run cross-country in the fall instead of playing in the marching band, which, at that time, had become his third alphabet. I was very pleased when Omari refused the suggestion.

At the end of the second quarter in ninth grade, however, he dropped to a C+ in science, and a C in English. I wrote in red ink to his teachers: "I am very concerned because I asked that you please call me half way through the second quarter if Omari was not improving. He went down in three areas, and you never called. I wish to have a conference as soon as possible!" Jerri and I went to the school and raised hell with both the teachers and the principal. We left only after I threatened to bring my concerns to a school board meeting, and after having obtained assurances of their strict attention to Omari's performance from his teachers. Several weeks later, one of them responded with a formal "academic deficiency report": "Dear Mr. Daniel: Omari is too interested in entertaining the class to pay attention to me. What would you have me do now?" Despite what I sensitively took to be a racial jab at me for having raised a "natural born entertainer," I wrote back: "Thank you for your concern, and its immediate expression to me. You don't have to do anything. His mother and I will handle the matter. I can assure you that his entertaining days are over."

I decided that Omari's conduct required drastic action on my part. Too many young black males were going down too many blind paths; even with proper guidance, my son seemed to be veering toward academic detours that led to nowhere. I was not going to have my son travel any of those routes even if, as my father had always said to me, I had to "half kill" him. Because he was in ninth grade and no longer a child receiving spankings, I was prepared to give Omari an old fashioned, get down lesson with my belt—until Jerri called a technical foul on me by inquiring gently, "Jack, what about what your first-grade teacher did to you?"

Jerri didn't want me to hit Omari, and didn't believe in beating children under any circumstances, but I couldn't believe she stooped so low to get her way. She had gotten my first-grade report card out of my high school yearbook and was now waving it in my face. I had always considered this teacher to be a racist who had set me up and then didn't have the heart to go through with her dirty deeds. When I was in first grade, teachers only recorded an S for "satisfactory progress", and an X for "pupil needs to show greater progress in order to reach the standard required." After the first twelve-week period, my teacher gave me an X in everything. After the second twelve-week period, she gave me an X in everything. The fact that I managed to earn an S in everything for the final period and pass to second grade was proof to me that she had been biased for two-thirds of the academic year. Jerri's analogy had to be false; Omari's teacher was trying to help him, and Omari wouldn't listen to his teacher, Jerri, or me. I knew that my teacher had had it in for me.

After explaining all of this to Jerri, she said in a disturbing voice, "Jack, did it ever occur to you that she passed you because you were black, and she didn't want you in her class for a second year? If she did, then neither your brains nor your father's beatings did you as much good as you seem to believe."

I considered this, but I didn't answer her as I proceeded upstairs to get my belt. When I came back down, Jerri barked in staccato, "Don't-hit-Omari-with-that-belt!" Seeing the fire in my eyes, she backed down a bit, asking, "Why don't you try to talk to him? Have you ever thought of listening to his explanation?" Past reason now, I screamed, "Jerri, I have tried talking, and look at the good it produced! Omari needs to be torn up the way Daddy beat me!"

As I hit him the first time, my fury was transformed into the sickening feeling of beating myself. When I hit him the second time, my arm movement was slowed by my suddenly rising fear, clearly related to my first-grade report card. My mind raced through the negative effects failing would have had on me. I thought about the possibility that, while repeating first grade, I would have been the class clown just like big, ugly Jonathan who had failed first grade and repeated it in my class. My mind flashed over to the teacher's comments on Omari's deficiency report. The anxiety intensified as my fears for Omari intermingled with my fears for my child-self. I realized that I wouldn't have gone on to second grade with my two closest friends, George and Herbie. Our "Three Rocket Boys" space-traveling group would have been split; they might have replaced me with someone like Charles, one of the fastest runners in our grade. My girlfriend Nadine probably would have dropped me for some second-grade big shot. It was bad enough when she started to like that jive-time T. J., the midget-league quarterback.

I thought about the fact that several of Omari's African American friends had failed a grade. I wondered what it was like for him to make friends with the white students in our primarily white suburban neighborhood. Had Omari's own "Rocket Boys"-type relationships been split up? Was his conduct a way of rebelling and identifying with his friends of color? It was horrible to think that for Omari, passing might have social consequences as dire as failing the first grade would have had for me.

I think I hit Omari for only a third or fourth time, and stopped as I got caught up in these thoughts. As I reflected on Jerri's words, I could

not imagine that being whipped about my X marks in first grade had produced a positive influence on me. My mind and emotions boiled with
guilt for having whipped Omari, anger for the whippings I did receive
for school-related reasons, and anger at the teacher—this time for probably passing me when I did not deserve to pass, and the fact that she might
have saved my life.

Regardless of the emotional maelstrom it had produced in me,
Omari's whipping seemed to have helped some because, during the final
quarter, he earned several A grades and only one grade less than a B, and
that grade was a C+, still in English. Now, though, I was unable to feel
satisfied completely with his progress because I had come to focus on the
idea that his teacher, too, might have done what was necessary to get rid
of her "entertainer of the year."

My fear and battle for Omari's survival continued. When he was in senior
high school, Omari nearly threw a tantrum when I asked him to write an
essay for the local Martin Luther King, Jr. "I Have a Dream" contest. I
had hardly finished what seemed to me to be a reasonable request before
he began with, "Daddy, every year you ask me to do the same old thing.
I've written about him and his dream every year. I know, I know. He had
this dream. He believed that everybody should love everybody, and judge
people by the content of their character, and . . ." Since he was talking
back to me, doing what my mother called "sassin'" me with his "man-
nish self," I interrupted with, "Omari, be quiet and write the essay!" The
way he was talking, rolling his eyes, and gesturing wildly reminded me
of just why the "old school" told children, "If you don't listen, you are
going to feel; a hard head makes a soft behind." He pushed at me again.

"What do you want me to write that I haven't already written?"

"Do what I told you to do before I hurt you! Just write it!"

With that, he left the family room in a huff. As he sat down at the
dining-room table, he mumbled something just loud enough for me to

hear about "this stupid writing." Since he had at least gotten started, I didn't say anything else to him. In his usual "just do enough to satisfy the basic request from Daddy" mode, Omari handed me an essay in about twenty minutes. I refused to read it; as I handed it back, I told him to do a careful review of it and then produce it on the computer.

A few weeks later, as I came in from work one day, Omari rushed up to me excitedly.

"Daddy, Daddy, guess what? I won!"

"You won? What?"

"I won the Martin Luther King essay contest! I'm getting a plaque and one hundred dollars for first prize from the Black Child Development Institute!"

I could not believe this young Negro. Omari hadn't won a thing. If I hadn't made him write that essay, this "win" never would have occurred. He failed to remember the fuss he had made; he had all but blasphemed King's name. As I viewed it, I was the one who had won by making him write the essay, and to make my point, I told Omari he had to give me half of the money. He protested, screaming that the money was his.

"Your money? Who made you write the essay?" He retorted sassily, "Well, who is going on television to read their essay?"

"I don't care who is going on which television station to read which essay. I just want my half of the money."

This scene reminded me of a story my father-in-law liked to tell about a man winning at the track, so I decided to try to illustrate my point by telling it to Omari.

"Listen. A man went to the racetrack with his entire paycheck. He lost five races in a row, and was down to the last twenty-five dollars of his pay. He knew his wife was going to kill him since this would be the second month in a row that they couldn't pay their bills. So, the man prayed for God to send him a sign. When the man lifted his head and looked out on the track, he saw one gray horse whose color he took to be a sign from God. The problem was that the horse was going off at ninety-nine to one odds. Since he had prayed for a sign from God, the man decided to show his faith in God by putting his last twenty-five dollars on this ninety-nine to one shot.

When the horses came out of the gate, the gray horse was dead last, and so the man prayed earnestly for God to help the horse. 'Lord, this is old Leroy calling on you. I know that the gray horse isn't much, but I know that all power is in your hands. Lord, would you please use a little of your spare power on that horse for me today?' When the horses went around the first turn, the gray horse was still last, and the man started praying heartily about how he was going to attend church every Sunday, quit drinking, quit smoking, and get to work on time every day. Then the man added, 'And Lord, if you let this horse win, I will never return to the racetrack. Please Lord, let him win. Let him win, Lord.' Suddenly, the gray horse started to gain ground. As the gray horse gained on the others, the man started yelling, 'Go ahead, Lord! Go ahead, Lord! Do your thing, Lord! You the man, Lord!' When the horses turned the last corner and headed toward the finish line, the gray horse was in front by five lengths. Suddenly the man cried, 'Okay Lord, okay Lord, I can take it from here myself!' And off he went to the window to collect his winnings."

He laughed throughout the telling, and when I ended, his devilish grin made me believe that Omari had gotten the point of the story. He was going to collect "his" money, read "his" essay on TV, because "he" had won; he was going to take it from here himself. I just couldn't permit Omari to think that he had really won. I could not let him forget how I'd had to make him write the essay, or his ill-behaved efforts not to do so. More importantly, I didn't want him to think that he had now achieved the essential level of writing excellence that he needed as a black male in American society. I thought of my mother's adage, "When success goes to a man's head, it leaves him looking in the wrong direction." I decided to turn Omari's head back in the right direction.

"OK, I'll tell you what. Since you now write so well, this weekend I want you to write an essay on Malcolm X."

"Aw, Daddy! Why?"

I answered him with something my father always said to me.

"Because it will do you some good."

True to his developing form, Omari asked, "Did the Lord make the gambler bet again to do him some good?"

"Go write," I responded quickly so that Omari wouldn't think that he had gotten the best of me. I was shocked by his question and its implied answer; only after he had left the room wearing a smile did my own face relax into one, too. I had to admire the quickness of his wit.

Throughout the rest of high school, Omari took care of business, earning mostly A grades, doing especially well in science courses and in the marching band. He continued to have problems with writing, however. He tried to dodge a twelfth-grade required essay on *Macbeth* by instead producing a video he called "MacRapper." While I had to admit that the video was impressive, and that I was proud of his creativity and his teacher's praise, I also made him write the essay. Although the content was pretty good, it contained spelling errors; he protested when I told him to run it through the computer's spell check and print another copy. He just did not seem to "get" my fears about what could happen to him as an African American male, irrespective of his achievements. He thought I was nagging him, being "the professor." Why couldn't he see what I was trying to do for him?

The struggle continued into college as he fussed and fumed about his "unfair" composition instructors. He was taking a wide range of subjects, a number of which were in literature. At least once a semester Jerri and I asked him about his plans for an academic major but he consistently responded, "Stop bothering me. I don't know yet." Shock cannot begin to describe my reaction when in the fall of his junior year, Omari declared a creative writing major. When I asked him why, he casually replied, "I had to choose something to graduate; most of my courses were in creative writing." I immediately assumed that he had simply taken an easy way out regarding his choice of major. I wondered if I would ever succeed in getting him to think seriously about the long-term impact of his educational decisions. Then I said to myself something I often heard my mother say in exasperation regarding me, "I'll just have to give him up into the hands of God!"

I found out more about his creative writing from one of his professors, who had supervised him as he wrote a collection of poems entitled "We Fish." I was dumbfounded as she told me about the "fascinating poems" Omari had written, but I thought she was simply being nice because I had helped recruit her as a faculty member. Also, since I suspected the presence of the often-articulated view that African American women tend to "raise our girls and spoil our boys," I thought that she was being a little soft with Omari. Perhaps most of all, though, I just didn't believe Omari was serious about his choice of poetry as his area of emphasis.

I had always found it difficult to appreciate poetry and the poetic form—to know when a poem was a poem and when a poem was just someone's strangely arranged words in structures known and understood only by them. Sometimes I even wondered whether poems were written by people like Omari who I thought were too lazy to write complete sentences, although I must admit to having tried to write poems myself but never doing better than the most elementary rhymes. What further aroused my suspicion was my awareness of how much Omari had gotten into rap music, which he claimed contained deep messages beyond what I perceived to be the usual misogynistic, sexually explicit, violent lyrics littered with "niggers," "motherfucking" this, and "motherfucking" that.

However, when I read another collection of his poems, I was moved to understand that Omari had used writing as an effective way of handling life's traumas.

Greek Picnic

Philly
My people jamming
with my people
A rainbow of chocolate
looming through the streets
Instinctively being pushed along
by a soulful bass-filled rhythm

My people were around me
My people were with me
then without missing a beat
They were shooting
My people were shooting
at my people
they ran to, from, and around me,
and I too ran
ran and hid from my people

There my sister lay
more dark African blood
spilling into American soil

This time the cause wasn't

Those people
It was my people
I did not stop to help
my sister because
my people were still shooting
at my people
and I was alone

Dealing with That Time

That time when you had me in your basement
where empty pop cans decorated the walls.
That time when I was too young to know better
but old enough to remember.
That was the time you took down my pants,
saying that you had a game for me.
You put your warm lips on my penis.
You said you were making it grow.
I remember you looking up into my face,
your eyes did not lie, so I didn't panic,
didn't fight, didn't enjoy, or at least I don't
think that I did. I just stood silent.

I had it all planned for the next time I saw you.
I began lifting weights, you were seven years
older than me, I needed strength. I practiced
for you. I punched my pillow, I punched the sofa,
I punched the walls, I was going to punch you.
You were going to fall. You would not fight back,
just lie there and know why you were bleeding.

I have seen you several times since then,
and I haven't punched you.
The image of you lying there
mouth bleeding is so sweet to me. I could
not swing. I was arthritic around you,
joints would freeze, muscles rebel, mind unwind.

When your brother got asthma, I went out and laid
in a field of freshly cut grass and watched the day pass.
When your father died, I went fishing with my father,
and we seemed to have caught more smallmouth bass
that day than ever before. I made sure to kiss him, that night
you wept for your father, and tell mine how much I loved him.

When your stepmother got laid off, I went to work with my mother
and played Duck Duck Goose with the children at the center.
I read to them, chuckled as I envisioned the lady my mother fired
as your stepmother. When you were accused of molesting another
child, I binged on a four-course meal. I had golden brown
turkey, prime rib, corn bread, scalloped potatoes, shrimp,
black-eyed peas, and for dessert triple-layer chocolate cake
and deep-dish apple pie. When you were acquitted, I purged
myself. I puked up all that I had enjoyed. I tried to throw up all
my memories. I thought of your eyes that
never betrayed you and wanted to vomit in them. I wanted to get
it out, get you out, but I couldn't. Now I am waiting to see you,
I hope I don't freeze, I hope I can end my silent rage.

When I finished reading "Dealing with That Time," my rational facul-
ties gave way to one of the most nauseating feelings I have ever experienced. It stirred in my stomach, anxious to rush up my throat so that I,
too, could vomit. I knew the poem's content had to be true because I recognized the actual "basement where empty pop cans decorated the
walls," and my mind flashed back to that year when Omari requested
weights as a Christmas gift. My hurt feelings obtained no relief from recalling that the perpetrator had been raised in a single-parent home and
sexually abused by his stepmother. And the hurt I felt was for more than
Omari; it was for the perpetrator, the perpetrator's family, and for the
deep dismay I knew Jerri and Marijata would experience upon reading
Omari's lines of verse, and for not having known about the incident for
so many years. I became silent in an effort to absorb the pain.

As difficult as it was to learn for the first time of these disturbing experiences, my silence was not simply a function of my dismay. The poem
had convinced me that, to the extent that one can do so, Omari had managed this darker-side-of-life episode. So much of an African American
male's life could be determined by the way he dealt with violence in its
many manifestations. Becoming neither a victim nor perpetrator of vio-

lence was a key to African American male survival, and my mind seized again on the fact that Omari had used writing as an effective coping mechanism.

"Dealing with That Time" moved me in the ways that I had always thought written expression should move people. I always believed that it had to do something for you, had to move you in some fundamental fashion. The writing had to conjure up deep emotions, and make the emotions come alive deep within oneself; it had to present vivid accounts of personal, but shared, human experiences. Because this poem affected me in the way I thought a good piece of writing should, it stood as affirmation of Omari's talent as a writer. Still, I had to ask if this was merely wishful thinking; maybe my emotion came only from the truth behind the words, not the words themselves and Omari's skill in expressing them. I chose to ask him about the truth of the episode, which he confirmed. Psychologically, I felt as though I, too, had frozen before ending my silent rage. I felt the need to keep the content of "Dealing with That Time" to myself, although I was anxious for an evaluation of my son's work by some of my professional writer friends.

I started thinking about how I could have missed the poetic within Omari, and about how I might have missed his ability to resolve complex problems, including those about which I had so many lurking fears. What had he been thinking during my lectures? When he remained silent, as I had directed, what was he really thinking about my pushing him, beating him, and goading him? I had nearly tunnel vision when it came to my focus on teaching him to cope with societal problems, but I never thought about how he was coping with me, his father. Feeling quite uncomfortable about what I might have missed about Omari, I was reminded of the time as a child I couldn't see what my friends Mabel and Bee Bee claimed to be a "man on the moon." Moving on this memory, I wrote three or four pages of rambling prose from which Omari distilled the essence of the experience.

couldn't see for lookin

In grade school,
I kept hearing
know-it-alls
like Mabel
and Bee Bee
talk about seeing
some man on the moon
and one night
as I stood with them
staring up at the sky
I couldn't see
and still didn't believe,
but as they pointed and giggled
my eyes drifted
up Mabel's shadow
and I could see
that her legs
looked like two of the world's
most beautiful
dark brown baseball bats
with ankles
just thin enough
for a firm grip,
and legs that got nice and thick
just below her knees
and I could see
that Mabel's butt
looked like two of those curved
salt cured
Virginia hams
that Uncle William brought by
on Sundays.
Later, when we walked,
I watched as

Mabel's hams
pushed each side of her skirt
up and down,
allowing me to see
inch by inch
of her deep chocolate thighs
until finally
I thought I saw
what my buddy Otis called

that "wonderful stuff,"
and it was,
and I felt wonderful
until I looked up at the moon,
and saw him
looking down on me
seeing what I saw
seeing what I felt
and seeing that now
I was too ashamed
to look back
at that wonderful stuff.

The clearer the face became over the next two nights, the more I couldn't understand how I had missed it before. I felt so ridiculous that I never did let Mabel and Bee Bee know what I had finally seen. Similarly, I wasn't sure I could let Omari know what I had seen in him. What if it had been there all along, and I had missed it just as I had missed the man on the moon? I wondered what would I have learned if, instead of summarily silencing him and directing him, I had listened to whatever was going to follow, "But Daddy, I . . . ?" I just could not admit to the possibility that all of my efforts at chiseling him into a black man could have been more effective if I had worked, in less intrusive ways, with what was always there. I couldn't get past the fact that when it came to something I deemed necessary for his survival, my approach was uncompromising.

I mused about other ways I "couldn't see for lookin" and may have missed seeing below the surface of my own son. Maybe, I needed to look again, much more carefully, at the person I thought I had seen so clearly. Maybe, I needed to listen more carefully to Jerri when she said, "Jack, leave Omari alone. Don't try to rush him into manhood. He is going to be okay."

THE FEVER

OMARI CAME home from college for the Thanksgiving holiday, and seeking time alone to talk with him, I asked him to go with me to pick up the turkey. What I really wanted was a chance to ask about the Father's Day letter he had sent to me. As we headed to the car, he jokingly offered, "Let me drive, you're getting older now and need me to get you around." Without hesitating or saying a word, I handed him my car key. As soon as we left the driveway, I casually said, "I really enjoyed that Father's Day letter. It left me sky-high for days, but there was this one part that I didn't understand."

"What's that?"

"You wrote something about me having the fever when it comes to fishing. What did you mean by that?"

"You don't know, as bad as you get the fever? You should see yourself."

"What do you mean?"

"As soon as you say we're going fishing, it's like you've been put under a spell. You start talking faster, running off at the mouth, and what is really funny is that you remind me of the way Grandma talks and talks. Plus, an hour before we're supposed to leave, you're checking and rechecking stuff you'd loaded in the car the night before. And then, you drive like you're crazy, speeding all the way to the river."

Wanting to hear more because I thought he was confusing my excitement with a fever, I briefly explained, "I just want to get to the river because I'm anxious to fish." That really got him going.

"Sure, you fish all right. Did you ever stop to think about how long we're out there on the water, like from six or seven in the morning until noon? We load the fish into the ice chest. All morning, you've been handling slimy worms, stinking hellgrammites, and bleeding fish, but you grab your sandwich without having washed your hands. Then you gobble it down in about four bites as you're driving to the next spot. I hardly have time to finish eating before you're pulling off the road to fish again. You claim your arthritic knees are bothering you, but down over the steep hills you go to the river, pushing through tree branches and plowing through tall weeds and vines with stickers, as if they were not there."

"Well, even if I hurry to get there, at least I relax on the water."

"No, then we're back out there, wading and fishing until late in the evening, whether the fish are biting or not. It doesn't seem to matter to you how hot it is, how bad the mosquitoes are, or if it rains. It doesn't matter whether you catch one or a hundred fish! The only things that I've seen drive you off that river are lightning when it finally got close enough and darkness when it actually had the nerve to get dark. And when you are driving back from fishing, Daddy, you talk more than Grandma. On and on you go about this fish and that fish and what you plan to do the next time you fish here or there."

"So, that's what you call the fever?"

"What would you call it?"

"Love of fishing."

"Okay, call it what you want, but I call it the fever."

Not wanting to get into an argument, I said no more, still thinking he was confusing my love of fishing with what he called the fever. Mostly, I couldn't believe he had the audacity to compare my fishing to my mother's mind-numbing verbal assaults. And so I said no more as we drove to the grocery store. However, two weeks after Thanksgiving, something clicked when, without a comment, he sent me "Old Words." Immediately, the comparison between me and my mother, as well as the connection with the fever, became clearer.

Old Words

I can remember sitting in the kitchen not listening
to what my grandmother was telling me,
she would talk in a continual drone
starting with "baby, get you something to eat"
then offering me a soda or some cider
that The Tyler Boy brung by
all while telling me how my cousin So and So
just graduated, and his or her mamma
is at the hospital visiting the Reverend
"you know, sister Green's husband"
who preached about Abraham on the same Sunday that
that father was in the paper for beating his wife
"see, here's the clipping"
she would pull it from her apron
along with the handful of other clippings
that she was now telling the stories behind
"now ain't this a shame . . ."
I know she kept talking but
I would drift off like my father and her other children
taught me to do, making sure to say "uh-huh"
every few minutes or so
to give the appearance of listening
without being distracted by her sound
now that she is eighty-three
my grandmother doesn't have much to say
between her naps and she sits quietly while we talk
in her kitchen or around the tree at Christmas

every so often she chuckles at us
and makes a brief comment
the closest person to her quickly asks, "huh?"
to which she answers,
"You hear what I say"

After I read "Old Words," memories surfaced about how my mother would start talking and ramble through a string of unconnected events. During the most excruciating of those verbal marathons, even she seemed to be listening more to the sound of her voice than to what she was saying. I grew up believing "talking just to hear yourself talk" was invented for Mama. Yet, because of how we were raised during the late 1940s and early 1950s, none of her children dared to do anything but listen in anguish.

As a child, I often thought of Mama as a talking newspaper, repeating and elaborating upon the current events of the Johnstown African American community, the local crime scene in particular, and the "terrible goings on" of whoever occupied the White House at the time. Mama always talked about writing her book, and although she periodically jotted down notes, she stuck to literally telling her story. Sometimes her monologues were mixed with short riffs of church gossip; others with verbal whippings for how "low down, nasty, and dirty" one of her children had behaved in school or church. When she was angry, Mama's monologues were highly acidic, shredding my emotions as effectively as she shredded cheese with her hand-held metal grater. My emotions got mangled even more when her tirades were aimed at Daddy.

My father was a railroad man who lived in public housing, went to church every Sunday, and did things like build his own home during his spare time. Despite his best efforts and the fact that he treated her as though she were the queen bee, Mama reserved some of her most emotionally draining monologues for letting Daddy know that "ends still weren't being met." One day when Daddy came home dog tired from working a double shift on the railroad, Mama started right in on him.

"Russell, I don't want to be like the Joneses, get our heat cut off in the dead of winter, and have folks talking about us in the street. These children will catch their death of pneumonia if the company cuts the heat off. So you'd better get the gas bill paid. And we ain't going on welfare to do it, because I ain't never been on welfare in my life, and I don't intend to start now. Mama and Papa didn't raise me that way. If I need to, I can always go and get me a few days working for Miz Smith or some other white folk up in Westmount. She doesn't pay but five dollars a day and carfare, but it adds up after a few days. So you let me know what you're going to do about this gas bill because Phillis has got to have a new church dress, the way she is growing. Sterlin said that those old shoes of Russell Jr.'s are hurting his feet, and Jack Lee's shoes are run down and have holes in the soles. Something has got to be done about them children's shoes, with all of this snow on the ground, and I need enough money to get them at the Penn Traffic department store. I don't put nothing but the best on my children."

Mama always insisted on her children "having the best money could buy," no matter how long it took her to save the money, and even if it meant getting a new pair of shoes long after the old pair was worn out and hurting your feet from being too small. This particular evening, she shifted from our need for new shoes to her participating financially in church affairs.

"Russell, we just can't go on like this. I don't know why you don't listen to me. And Reverend Jefferson is looking for me to put ten dollars in the plate on Women's Day. He asked all of the Missionary Circle members to pay ten dollars each, and I intend to pay mine. I missed paying five dollars for the building fund campaign, but one way or another, I plan to participate for Women's Day. So something has got to be done, and I told you that last week."

Daddy sat in silence until Mama paused for no apparent reason; then, with his usual terseness, said, "Grace, you let me attend to all of that. I don't have a single bill that you need to worry about. I know just what needs to be done with them and the church's fund raising. Now hush, I am tired of all this talk about bills."

He returned to his conspicuous silence, and that was as close as Mama and Daddy came to arguing, at least in front of us. Mama would always have her long say, and then Daddy would add a short remark or two, ending the "discussion," and retreating into a murky silence which both frightened and saddened me. Often as she repeated herself over and over, Daddy sat staring silently or noisily turning the pages of the newspaper. We children sat at ringside, each receiving the emotional impact of the verbal blows being inflicted upon our father. I always felt so much better when Daddy used his deep, strong, commanding voice to utter a curt comment, and call a halt to Mama's monologues. I can still hear him saying, "Complaint, complaint, complaint! Grace, that's all I ever hear from you no matter what I do. Stop it, I'm tired!"

And she always stopped. I loved it when he made Mama stop because he was the only one who could stop her from talking before she had decided to on her own. I was tired, too. I was tired of her complaining regardless of what Daddy or any of the rest of us did. I was also tired of my strong hero father taking so much of what I viewed as undeserved abuse. He was so strong that once, when I didn't get off the floor as soon as he told me to do so, he grabbed me by the back of my coat, and picked me off the floor with one hand. There was nothing around the house that he couldn't lift, and other steelworkers talked about how Daddy could lift railroad equipment that none of them could lift alone. He had been a ferocious high school football player, and I couldn't understand why he let Mama go on blitzing him and us with her words. I often wondered if his silence was some price he decided to pay for her silence about some horrible deed on his part. I also wondered if, in the midst of so many other difficulties, her talk was just something he decided to bear for the sake of holding our family together.

But Mama also crocheted. It was after reading Alice Walker's critical essay "In Search of Our Mothers' Gardens" that I asked my eighty-year-old mother why she crocheted so much, though by then I suspected I knew. Mama sighed deeply, smiled, and said, "You don't know son, but there were times around the house when things weren't so good between your Daddy and me, and I prayed to God, and it seemed like not even God would help me. So when praying didn't help, I would get my needle and thread, sit down, and just do what came to me. Sometimes my hands would get to going so fast that I didn't know what I was doing. Then, about an hour later, I would look at what I had crocheted, and say, 'If that ain't something.' Then, it seemed like everything was going to be okay. You don't know what all Mama been through, son, and crocheting helped a whole lot." I certainly didn't know what all Mama had been through, but maybe I understood what the vehicle for her own healing and creative forces was.

Thinking further about "Old Words" also took me to a psychological space that I didn't really want to enter, leaving me feeling quite uncomfortable with myself as a father. Did Omari want me to understand my fever, in part, because he had remained silent when I had blitzed him with complaint, complaint, complaint about his schoolwork and other matters? Was that abuse too, abuse he accepted to keep our relationship together? Was writing for Omari what crocheting had been for Mama? Maybe this was why he said to me, "What you really need to do is write about your childhood, and then maybe you would understand your fever and a whole lot more."

Growing up, my life's circumstances were not as harsh as those of children living in the midst of gangs, crack cocaine, and drive-by shootings. However, although there were only four children at that time, six people living in a small, two-bedroom, segregated public housing unit was tough. Since I was the youngest, Sterlin and Russell made me sleep in the middle of our bed made for two. The person in the middle got a double dose of bad morning breath, suffered the most from what we called "good night" farts, and got rolled on as the other two tossed and turned during the night. I thought nothing was worse than sleeping in the middle on a hot, humid July night when none of us had taken a bath before going to bed. I was happy to get put out of the middle when Russell Jr. made me sleep on the side of the bed against the wall because my peeing in the bed caused both him and Sterlin to wake up cold, stinking, and wet. Then Sterlin had to sleep in the middle because, as the oldest person, Russell Jr. got to sleep on the outer edge of the bed. Our sister Phillis was the only sibling to have her own bed.

Without anyone telling us what to do, my older brothers and I got jobs as soon as we could while attending junior high school. Jobs got you money, along with status among your friends; just as importantly, jobs got you out of the house. Sterlin shined shoes, sold pop at Point Stadium baseball games, delivered newspapers, spotted pins in the bowling alley, and worked as a caddy on weekends at the Sunehanna Country Club. Russell Jr. worked after school and all day Saturday as a stock boy in the Style Store. We teased him because part of his job was to dress female mannequins. I sold potato chips and peanuts at the Point Stadium base-ball games, which I didn't much like; so eventually I turned to selling newspapers in my neighborhood and collecting scrap metal at the Beth-lehem Steel dump. By the end of junior high school, I, too, was working four nights per week in the bowling alley.

Mama took half of everyone's pay, except for Sterlin's, to "help out around the house." Sterlin always figured out a way to keep most of his money. Part of his deal was that he bought some of his clothing; by tenth grade, all of us earned enough to buy our back-to-school clothing. As teenagers, we each earned enough money to purchase our Easter outfits. Daddy said Easter was about "death and salvation," and so if we wanted to engage in what he called "form and fashion" on Easter Sunday, we had to put up our own money.

Since I was never able to see where my few dollars and cents went to helping out around the house, I resented Mama taking part of my money. I also didn't like myself for not having Sterlin's courage to argue successfully for keeping all of what I earned, particularly when I started buying just as much of my clothing as he did. I just surrendered my money on payday and ate my anger, the same way I did when Reverend Jeffer-son came to our house for dinner and seemed to care little, if at all, about our limited circumstances.

If he arrived on Sunday, Reverend Jefferson felt no shame eating most of the chicken breasts, which we considered to be the best parts. I can still hear his old, deep, frog-like voice saying, "Aw, Sis Daniel, you sure can fry up some chicken. From Georgia to Pennsylvania, I ain't never eaten any chicken better than yours, Sis Daniel. I believe that I'll have another one of those breasts if you don't mind." She would encourage him to eat as much as he wanted, dazzled by his oily flattery and buoyed by her sense of doing "God's work." "Help yourself, Reverend" became a phrase I detested.

During those Sunday dinner visits by Reverend Jefferson, I don't know who I disliked the most—him for eating all of that chicken or Mama for encouraging him to eat more. After he had eaten as though he didn't know that the Bible said it was a sin to be a glutton, Reverend Jefferson would sit in the living room with his hands folded over his stuffed and protruding stomach. I wanted to punch that stomach right below where his gold watch hung and make him throw up just like the time my friend Sinclair punched Raymond in the stomach right after Raymond had eaten lunch. It was so disgusting to watch Reverend Jefferson eat all of the best food and then sit in the living room, which was forbidden for me. I felt conflicted; though Mama always went on about her children having only the best, it seemed she cared more about our minister's perceptions of her as a good Christian woman than about the her children, who seldom had enough of anything. The worst part for me, though, was that Daddy allowed all of this to happen.

Johnstown summers were especially full of trouble as the stifling heat drove children and adults out of the hot, funky, brick buildings on hard-to-sleep nights. Girls got pregnant more often during the summer, and more guys got drunk on homemade Raisin Jack or Pluck over at Mr. Jones' pool hall. To keep us out of trouble during the summers, my parents sent my two older brothers and me "down home" as soon as school let out. Mama said being down home during the summer would keep us away from those bad Tyson boys and sassy Tyson girls, away from white troublemakers, and out of trouble in general. One day, about a week before my sixth-grade year ended, she told us, "All three of you need to stay away from those Tyson children. Those boys don't have an ounce of truth in them, and sooner or later, every one of them will wind up in the hands of the law. And you know they say that the oldest Tyson girl 'broke her leg' again. This will make the second baby that heifer has had in three years. That second baby is due in June, and who knows who she'll blame it on. So your Uncle John Henry is going to take you down home the first Saturday after you're out of school."

Daddy just said that it would "do us some good" to help out on the farm. I found it to be a limitless source for dispensing misery. Hot and humid only begin to describe steamy June, July, and August mornings in Elk Hill, Goochland County, Virginia where the Daniels, Youngs, and a few other families eked out a living. Down in Virginia, you had to get started by daybreak since, once the sun came up, you could work up a sweat just by walking. Mama's mother, Grandma Roni, made us wear straw hats so that we wouldn't get sunstroke and die.

As children, we got the job of "sloppin'" the hogs. For having to do this disgusting chore, sometimes we punished the hogs by peeing in the slop, or by beating the hogs with switches. We beat the hogs before we fed them so that Aunt Minnie and Uncle Youngie couldn't tell whether the hogs were squealing from the beatings or were just anxious to get to the slop. The buckets of slop often consisted of room temperature, vomit-like concoctions made of slick sticky watermelon rinds, bean shells, sour corn cobs, leftover food, stale moldy bread, sour milk, and much of what seemed to be just plain old garbage mixed with water.

We children also gathered and cleaned chicken eggs. Sitting around the table with a pan of warm water and a rag to clean the eggs served as a relentless reminder of just how chickens "laid" eggs. It was best to clean eggs early in the morning, before the heat of the day made the air in the room stand still. At that point, the odor crawled down your throat, slowly stirred your stomach, and almost made you gag. Despite the fact that we helped her earn her money, Daddy's stepmother, Grandma Kate, would not permit us to eat any of the eggs. Before we could ask, she would cackle, "Boys, boys, you know these eggs got to be sold in Richmond. Bring a good price. Yes indeed, bring a good price. If you're hungry, go in there and get some of those biscuits and pear preserves. Don't ever let me hear talk of you eating any of my eggs, you hear."

But sometimes Grandpa Daniel just didn't care about the price. He would say, "Kate, let the children have a few eggs." As Grandma Kate scowled, he told us, "Go on children. Eat all the eggs you want. Eat them until they run out of you." And we did; when we got the chance, we ate eggs like hungry raccoons that had broken into a hen house. However, these chances were few and far between; never-ending work was the normal routine.

Older guys plowed, and younger boys walked ahead of the plows, turning sweet potato vines out of the way so they would not be cut off by the plow. Your back felt like a stiff board after a morning of turning vines. We picked the green worms and pulled "suckers" (small shoots at the bottom of the plant) off the tobacco plants. For "fun," we thrashed wheat on the Fourth of July. Uncle Youngie would brag about how many more bushels of wheat he had produced than his neighbors. The day was completed with a big meal cooked by Grandma Kate. On the Fourth, even she let us eat some of those Richmond eggs. Whether it was pulling suckers, turning vines, milking cows, slopping hogs, hauling manure, getting firewood, or chopping weeds, there was always more work to do down home.

On Saturday evenings, if company was expected on Sunday, we swept the front yard using brooms made from bushes. I never disliked chickens and dogs so much as when we swept their waste from that yard. Later on, if Aunt Minnie caught you sitting around the house, she would send you on a quarter-mile walk down the hill to the spring. One evening, just before dark, she saw us sitting in the red sand under the towering black walnut tree, and she screamed, "Get up from there you nasty, good-for-nothing, lazy devils. You know I need some cooking water, and we need water to wash up with in the morning. Get every damn one of those empty buckets, and go down to the spring."

There was no thought of "pay" for working on the farm, although I did get fifty cents each time a truckload of pulpwood was sold. We cut pulpwood when the crops didn't demand our time; one summer, I made two dollars and fifty cents. That was the same summer that my brother Russell Jr. revolted, refusing to work, hiding in the bundles of wheat that had been stacked like a tepee. Even after Grandma Kate slapped him several times and withheld a drink of ice water, Russell Jr. refused to work that day. I thought that he was staging a general work stoppage based on the heat and the hard nature of the work. I learned more at lunchtime after Russell Jr. refused to eat any of Grandma Kate's cookies. Before we went back to work, I asked him why, and he said, "Come on down to the barn. I want to show you something. Wait until you see what is in those barrels."

When we got to the barn, there was a strong sweet smell coming from the oak barrels. Russell Jr. lifted a lid off one, and I saw the same cookies that Grandma Kate had been feeding us. Angrily, Russell Jr. said, "See, Grandma Kate has been feeding us some of the hogs' cake feed. They picked up these old, cracked cookies after they sold the eggs in Richmond. She's been feeding us the ones with only a small piece broken off and with no mold on them, and the hogs have been getting the rest of the cake feed mixed into their slop."

That evening the poor hogs paid for Grandma Kate's sins as we beat them harder than we usually did when we fed them. We beat the hogs instead of saying anything to our adult relatives because, back then, children didn't "talk back" to adults even when the adults were wrong. Plus, in this instance, no one would have believed us. Our nice, hardworking, religious grandmother just wouldn't have done a thing like that. It was hard enough for me to believe that she had been feeding us hog food. And it was even more disconcerting to even think that our wonderful Grandpa Daniel might have had knowledge of the deed.

Most of the time, I really couldn't see how Daddy thought helping out down home was doing us so much good. All that I saw was a lot of hard work, and I didn't know which was worse—hard times down in

Virginia or hard times up in Johnstown. What I did know was that we worked awfully hard down in Virginia just to keep out of trouble up in Johnstown. Thus, it was more than special when on some Saturdays or Sundays, Russell Jr., Sterlin, and I took a ten-minute walk down to the "branch," a little creek meandering through the lowest end of the cow pasture.

During the summer, the deepest part of the creek was about two feet and it was almost eight feet wide. When it rained, the branch would run muddy red and rise so high that cars could no longer cross. Throughout most of the summer, though, it was crystal clear, and, most importantly, full of minnows. We used the slop buckets to go fishing for minnows. Barefoot and in nothing but our ragged shorts, we tiptoed quietly through the water trying not to scare the minnows. Then we stood still and waited for the minnows to swim near us, and with a quick dip of our buckets, tried to scoop them up. Water splashed everywhere, providing a refreshing feeling almost as much fun as catching the minnows. We fished for hours, and if it wasn't for Aunt Minnie calling us, we might never have quit.

While fishing at the branch, I was through with the troubles of the world: the pain of hearing Mama talk again about unpaid bills, the misery of sleeping in cramped, musty, project bedrooms, the drudgery of always working very hard in Johnstown and down home, and the constant, unwanted supervision of adults. During those moments in the water, I forgot about my desire for Daddy to use something other than a few stern words to end a discussion with Mama, and my dislike for him never having done so. The branch was a place where my fantasies came to life, and the mere thought of going there induced behavior that Omari later called signs of the fever.

Aunt Minnie didn't allow us to go down to the branch during certain days that she called "dog days." One July day when we were gathering our slop buckets and mason jars to go fishing, she told us, "You all stay out of that branch during these bad dog days. If you don't stay out of that water, you all will be full of ticks. Then Youngie is going to have to use that iodine and the tweezers to pick them out of you. If he doesn't get them ticks off of you in time, they'll kill you."

According to Aunt Minnie, dogs and wild animals went down to the branch to wallow and cool off during dog days. If we played in the branch at that time, we would get the ticks on us that were washed off the animals' bodies. Nevertheless, when Aunt Minnie and Uncle Youngie had gone over to Cartersville to shop for groceries, we went down to the water. After about an hour of fun, we went back to the house and made sure that we were completely dry before they returned. Later that evening, I felt a bump on my head, which I scratched constantly. Noticing my discomfort, Aunt Minnie said, "Boy, why are you scratching so much? Come here and let me look at your head." She held me by the neck, took one look at the spot I had been scratching, and screamed, "Lord, Youngie! This boy's head is full of ticks! Get the tweezers and iodine!"

Uncle Youngie sat me on the floor between his legs. I thought I had experienced real pain when Mama pinched me on the arm for not listening to her, but that was nothing compared to Uncle Youngie using the tweezers to pick at my scalp where the ticks had buried themselves. Since I kept jumping, he locked his knees around my head. Once a tick had been removed, he rubbed the spot with cotton soaked in iodine. It felt as though that part of my head had been set on fire. By the time the third and final tick had been removed, and I had received one last treatment of iodine in all three places, I thought I would never go back to the branch.

As I sat in the floor with tears streaming down my face, Aunt Minnie walked by and said, "I guess you'll stay out of that branch, you nasty little devil. I told you it was dog days. Now, go down there again if you dare." I looked on the floor at the pieces of cotton spotted with blood. I also saw the pieces of toilet tissue Uncle Youngie had used to smash the ticks, once he got them out of my head. The burning sensations returned briefly, and I pondered again whether I would ever go back to the branch. Deep down, I knew full well that I would.

We spent every hour we could fishing down at the branch. Every now and then, a two- or three-inch fish appeared in the deepest part, but we never were able to catch the big ones. From then on, I knew fishermen were not lying when they talked about the big one that got away. When we told Uncle Youngie about the big fish in the branch, he said, "Shucks, boys, the fish over in the James River are every bit of fifteen and sixteen inches long. Some of those channel cats go up to two feet. I can cut you a pole, put some line on it, get some bait, and you can catch all the big fish you want."

Anxiously, I asked Uncle Youngie if he would take us, but he answered distantly, "One day, I reckon, after we knock off from work." We never knocked off from work early enough to go fishing, since Uncle Youngie was always too busy working, or resting from having worked so hard.

Once, two of Mama's brothers, Uncle Nash and Uncle William, came down home for "Second Sunday" in August. This was the time of a big religious revival for colored people. My uncles went fishing on the James River while the rest of the folks were "going to the mourners bench," "getting converted," "seeking the Lord," "breaking the hold" that the Devil had on them, and "getting right with God." That night, when my uncles came back to the house, they had several long, gray catfish that were the length of Aunt Minnie's dishpans. The fish were still breathing in slow pants, they had a little blood trickling from their gills, and they wiggled when we jabbed them with a stick. I imagined the fun my uncles must have had catching those fish, and then I thought about how I had sat uselessly all night in that hot, sweaty church, never once feeling anything of a spiritual nature. Nor did I believe that the Devil had a hold on me. I just had Aunt Minnie holding me back from fishing.

All of the older relatives were disappointed because Sterlin and I didn't walk forward when the preacher "threw out the lifeline," hoping that all sinners would heed God's call. Russell Jr. had been baptized two years earlier, and Daddy and Mama had asked Uncle Youngie to see what he could do to get Sterlin and me "saved" that summer. We would be going home in a week, and neither one of us had shown a single sign of spiritual growth. One Friday, after we finished working, Uncle Youngie took us to the side of his truck and said in a solemn voice, "Jack Lee and Sterlin, I want you boys to think about putting God in your hearts. Tomorrow night, when Reverend Walker puts out the call, think about answering. Move on up front, and tell him you want the Lord Jesus Christ to be your personal savior. Just watch how the other young folk go about seeking the Lord, and do what they do." Knowing what was expected of me, I replied, "Yes sir, Uncle Youngie," but I was really angry and frustrated. Here he was again talking about spending time dealing with Jesus, and all I really wanted was to spend time fishing with Uncles Nash and William. When I asked to go fishing with them, Aunt Minnie made me more angry, frustrated, and curious, saying, "Boy, you don't need to go anywhere with Nash and William. The way they drink all that liquor and chase after women, Grace would kill me if she found out that I let you go off with them."

Realizing that Aunt Minnie wasn't going to let me go anywhere with my two uncles, I went outside and sat in the red sand under the big black walnut tree. Watching a bunch of tiny red ants push and pull a big, dead grasshopper, I thought about besting the larger adults by lying and doing just what Uncle Youngie said about accepting the Lord Jesus Christ into my heart. Next Tuesday night, I'd go right up to the front, keep chanting, "I love Jesus," and join the church. Maybe that would change Aunt Minnie's mind before my uncles went back to Johnstown. Despite my resolve, I fell asleep during the sermon that Tuesday night. I didn't wake up until the deacons were taking up the collection, missing both my chance to find Jesus and possibly to go fishing on the James River with my uncles.

Our "cousin" Bob (a foster child raised by Grandpa Daniel and Grandma Kate) did take my brothers and me fishing in a backwoods "fishing pond." After a very heavy rain, the creek on Grandpa Daniel's farm often overflowed its banks, leaving small "fishing ponds" in sunken wooded areas. One area had stagnant water about two feet deep, and it had about a twenty-five-foot oblong shape. When we got to this "fishing pond," Bob walked around the woods until he found a stick about the size of a base-ball bat, only longer. Then he waded into the water and asked, "What y'all standing there like big damn dummies for? Why don't you find a stick like mine and come on in this water? We're going to get these devils."

As we searched for sticks, Bob began to walk slowly through the moss, leaves, and other stuff floating on the stagnant water. As each of us joined him in the water, black water bugs zigzagged and water spiders glided across the surface. Bob began to stir the bottom of the "fishing pond" with his stick, saying, "Come on, do like you see me doing."

There we were, all in the water, stirring up a mess as if we were making a giant, muddy milk shake. Gradually the pond's surface turned into a muddy brown wave pool with moss, leaves, small sticks, and slime splashing everywhere. Suddenly, Bob smacked his stick on the surface of the water, and a struggling fish floated on the surface. Then he instructed, "Watch for the fish to come up for air, and then knock the shit out of them." We did, and water and gook flew everywhere. More and more fish began to float on the water's surface. We yelled and screamed, hitting the fish until there appeared to be no more alive. This felt even better than playing in the branch. In the midst of this frenzy, those little fish paid with their lives for all of that hard work I had to do down home, the times I didn't get to go to the James River, the times I had eaten hog food, and the times I had to seek Jesus instead of going fishing. I even beat memories of Daddy sitting in silence while Mama talked on and on. I was so caught up in this brutal but exhilarating cathartic experience that I didn't notice Bob when he got out of the water to cut a willow branch for stringing the fish.

As we sat by the edge of the water putting the fish on the willow branch, we saw one long, wounded fish swirling in an S-like pattern. The struggling fish drifted closer and closer to the edge of the water. Horrified, my brothers and I started running when the fish started crawling out of the water. We stopped running when we heard a low thud, followed by, "Got him. Get back here you city slickers. Goood goddamn! Boy, were y'all hauling ass!"

We turned, and saw Bob holding the tail of a monstrous water moccasin.

It had taken Omari's prodding to help me see why fishing did, and still does, give me the fever—though I never called it that. I loved fishing because it was everything that the Johnstown projects, down home hard work, and Mama's talking weren't. Fishing in the branch gave me a chance to escape, to let my mind flow out of a world that produced disquieting feelings and into an entirely different universe in which I would not be bothered by anything. It appears that the adrenalin rush associated with merely the thought of going fishing occurs because I know now, as I knew then, that I will soon experience something so internally satisfying that it will soothe my entire being. And having reflected on all of this, it also appears that there might have been something quite paradoxical for Omari about fishing with me.

Gradually, into my consciousness seeped the possibility that Omari escaped the pushing, driving, and molding of his father by fishing with him. When his overbearing father became afflicted with the fever and took him fishing, there came a chance for him to bond with a father who also just wanted to relax. Gone were the uncompromising concerns with developing mastery of writing and math skills, doing extra readings, and the various forms of stern guidance intended to save his son from real and imagined dangers. And fishing became the times for just "us" together, times I too cherished.

4

THE LITTLE RIVER

MAMA AND Daddy didn't have a car, and so relatives always came
down home to bring us back to Johnstown. Who came for us depended
on whose church was holding revival the third or fourth Sunday in August, and which of my uncles with cars could get off from work. Because
of small congregations, the African American churches took turns holding revivals in August. A revival was supposed to focus on God, but for
most people it was really a big family reunion and general social event.
Uncle Tom always said that, at revival time, "more corn liquor got
poured than communion wine." Aunt Sally claimed she didn't believe
in any "baptizing foolishness," because folks "went down as dry sinners,
and came up as wet sinners." After a weekend of sinners seeking and
finding God, adults enjoying their annual reunions, and children pic-
nicking and playing with seldom seen cousins, we headed back to Johnstown. It was a great way to end months of hard work.

At the end of the summer of 1954, Aunt Nancy and Uncle John
Henry came to get us. On the way home, their car's trunk was stuffed
with luggage, and there was a sack of corn and a huge salt-cured ham in

the front seat. Along with some clothing we couldn't fit into the trunk, I had to sit with my two brothers in the cramped back seat of their two-door, light green Pontiac. Actually, I was very pleased that I was too big to sit in the front on Aunt Nancy's lap during the almost eight-hour, cramp-producing ride. Mostly, I was glad to be going home.

Not even the pleasant thought of stopping in Breezewood to eat Aunt Minnie's crispy fried chicken, thick biscuits, heavily seasoned potato salad, and delicious, deep yellow pound cake took my mind off getting home. We always stopped at the Breezewood exit because going to Virginia, it was the last stop to get gas, and, returning, it was first public place in Pennsylvania where we would not experience racially segregated facilities. To this very day, as an act of remembrance, I stop at Breezewood each time that I travel the Pennsylvania Turnpike.

Starting junior high school that fall meant going downtown every day, eating in cafeterias, and being with the "big guys." Also, I couldn't wait to hear what I had missed all summer. I would find out who had gotten whom pregnant, who Josephine was going with after she dropped Jody the week before we left for Virginia, and who had been sent to reform school and for how long. The previous summer when I got back to Johnstown, everyone was talking about Bennie who had been sent to reform school for robbing old Mr. Solomon's shoe store. Also awaiting my return was a really good-paying job delivering the *Johnstown Tribune-Democrat* and earning a dollar and fifty-six cents per week. With this job, I would earn more weekly than I had ever made in my life.

I had fifty-two newspaper customers, one of whom was Mr. Rhinehart. One summer day, as I was saving time by cutting through Mr. Rhinehart's backyard, I noticed that he had recently come back from fishing. On the dark green grass in the shade of one of his big sour cherry trees, along with his fishing rods, he had placed about ten or twelve of what looked like the largest fish in the world. For longer than I can remember, I stood there admiring those dark bronze fish. Hearing his screen door open and seeing him come outside, I fired off,

"What kind of fish are they, and how did you catch them? How long did it take . . . ?

Mr. Rhinehart spit some tobacco juice and interrupted with, "Hold on Jackie. Let me take you fishing some time, and I'll answer your questions."

"Well, where did you catch them?"

"Over in the Little River, the branch of the Juniata River."

"I'd surely like to go with you, but I don't have a fishing rod."

Again before speaking, he shot some tobacco juice on the ground, and followed with, "Well, let me know when you get one, and I'll take you out with me one day."

He didn't realize it, but Mr. Rhinehart had offered me a chance to live out the dreams I had developed down at the branch. Catching just one fish like the ones he had caught would have been like the time that Santa Claus left me a six-shooter that sent curls of smoke into the air after each shot. All that I needed was a fishing rod to realize my dreams.

Luck was on my side. Several days after Mr. Rhinehart made his offer, the *Johnstown Tribune-Democrat* held a newspaper boy contest related to obtaining new customers. One possible prize was a fishing rod. I went door-to-door soliciting new customers, always prefacing my sales pitch with, "I am Deacon Daniel's son" or "Sister Grace's son." All over the city of Johnstown, and especially within my immediate neighborhood of Prospect, older people had a lot of respect for "Deacon Daniel," "Sister Grace," and God.

I got fifteen new customers, two more than what I needed to obtain my first fishing rod. Two weeks later when the shipment arrived, I picked up the fishing rod at the *Johnstown Tribune-Democrat's* downtown office and then rushed home to show it to my parents. From there, I went throughout the neighborhood showing the rod to all of my friends and anyone else who would look. I could hardly wait to take Mr. Rhinehart up on his offer to take me fishing.

The next day, I carried the rod, along with my sixty-seven folded papers in my paper sack, to show it to Mr. Rhinehart. He took a quick glance at my new fishing rod, and with a look of concern, he spit some tobacco juice and asked, "Heck, Jackie, where is the reel?"

My heart fell to my stomach with disappointment. No reel! I still couldn't go fishing. I had assumed that rods came with attached reels, and my excitement caused me to miss the obvious. Noting my dismay, Mr. Rhinehart said, "Wait a minute, I have one that I can sell you. I'll let you have it cheap. Just make sure that you keep it oiled."

With that advice, Mr. Rhinehart sold me my first reel for five dollars, with no down payment. The reel seemed to have been made of precious metals, since each side of the reel consisted of a shiny, burgundy metal with a gold swirl. I wondered a little about Mr. Rhinehart letting me take the reel with me, without a down payment, and permitting me to pay over time. I didn't know if he was doing me a favor, just trying to get rid of an old reel, or was naive about selling used things. Had I been dealing with anyone else, they would have made me pay some minimum deposit. Mr. Rhinehart didn't even ask me to pay him back ten cents on the dollar, the way Mr. Frenchy charged people when he loaned them money. Since he was so honest, I paid Mr. Rhinehart off as soon as possible, using some of his weekly tips to help pay for the reel.

I finished delivering my papers, rushed home, and went into the backyard to practice casting for the big one. I imagined one of Mr. Rhinehart's big fish swimming in the corner of the yard, behind a rock around which Daddy's roses were growing. To increase the difficulty of the cast, I pretended that the clothesline holding some of Daddy's gray work shirts was a tree hanging above the rock. As I swung the rod back in the clock-like position that I had once seen during the short segment before a feature Roy Rogers movie, I experienced that embarrassing feeling of having something obviously wrong while the whole world was watching. I discovered that reels did not come equipped with fishing line. I felt as though I had walked outside without my pants, and my hoped-for girl-friend, Nadine, who was still going with that quarterback, T. J., was standing in front of me.

Daddy gave me money to buy some fishing line, and as I was about to rush off to the store, he added, "I gave you enough money for hooks too. Get size fours." Oblivious of the more than a mile walk to and from the store, I hurried home to put on the line. With the reel loaded, I tied on one of the size-four hooks, and made a cast that dribbled to the ground about two feet in front of me. No one had to explain. I had forgotten the sinkers.

No problem! I knew just what to do for sinkers. There was no need to go back to the store. My father, two older brothers, and I were in the process of completing building the home in which we were living. "Finishing nails," used when you want to sink the head of the nail just below the surface of the wood, would work well. Since there were a lot of them and I didn't think Daddy would miss them, I took a handful. With a hammer and a pair of pliers, I bent them into loops that I could tie onto my line. Now I was finally ready to go fishing, and I could not wait for Mr. Rhinehart to decide on a date. The waiting was unbearable since we couldn't go until he was off from work on a weekend and I could find someone reliable to deliver my papers. Finally, one Friday afternoon, he said, "Jackie, if you can take off, let's go fishing tomorrow. Be here around six-thirty in the morning, and bring your bait."

With a force stronger than usual, I bounced my last paper off the side of my customer's home and onto his porch. About twenty minutes later, my friend George agreed to deliver my papers on Saturday. As I headed home to tell my parents that Mr. Rhinehart was taking me fishing, I worried about the fact that he told me to bring my bait. What kind of bait did you use? Where would I get it? Daddy saved the day.

He got a Crisco can out of the garbage can, cleaned it out, used a big nail to punch holes into opposite sides of the can, tied a piece of twine to each hole in the can, and smiled as he placed the twine over my shoulder. Then he grabbed his garden fork and said, "Come on."

Daddy dug up about twenty worms in his garden, and I put them into the Crisco can. I covered the worms with a handful of dirt, and as he added a handful of grass, he told me to sprinkle a little water on the grass to help keep the worms cool and moist. I was finally ready to go fishing.

Tossing and turning, each time that I checked the alarm clock, it seemed as though four-thirty would never arrive. When the alarm finally startled me, I jumped out of bed, dressed in minutes, and after a brief stop in the bathroom, gathered my things and headed for Mr. Rhinehart's house. I got there around quarter past five in the morning, and sat on his porch, in the dark, until I saw the light come on in his bedroom around six o'clock. As soon as I saw the light, I started knocking on his door. I needed to get off that creaky wooden porch because I could hardly wait to go fishing, and because I had already seen two unidentifiable objects move across the grass. One of the two objects, or possibly a third source, had made a strange snarling noise. It was none too soon when Mr. Rhine-hart came to the door, dressed in his underwear.

I stood there with my rod in one hand, and in the other, a brown bag containing a can of pop, two grape jelly sandwiches and an apple, which Mama said I needed to help "clean me out." The Crisco can of worms was hanging over my shoulder. My hooks and bent finishing nails were stuffed in my front pockets for easy access. For a fishing hat, I had borrowed one of Daddy's old blue- and white-striped work hats those railroad men wore. Why Mr. Rhinehart had started laughing was beyond me. I was ready to go fishing, I was at his house ahead of time, and he was late. Yet, there he was, standing in his red- and white-striped underwear, with his knobby red knees and pale white legs showing, and he was the one laughing? If only he could have seen how the color of his white legs didn't match his leathery, reddish brown face, he wouldn't have been laughing. I should have been the one laughing, given the way that his little round watermelon stomach was sticking out under his old-fashioned T-shirt.

So You Want to Learn to Fish?

Get up too early to see,
get your pants, shirt, then boots
into the car and drive too fast.
jump out and grab worms in your talons
grab a rod and chains
climb down through gnats, mud
ivy and sticker bushes
to the banks of life.
step into the cold water ecstasy
let your body go numb
let it sense a rock under the surface
cast into the current
let the bait drift to your dream
feel the tender taps
then lift your rod high
pump the reel, like you're not afraid
for the creature, mouth open,
to enter your stories.

It was a little more than an hour's drive to Bedford, Pennsylvania, through which flowed the Little River. The Saturday morning trip seemed to take all day, but I was too excited to sleep in Mr. Rhinehart' blue-green Chevy. Although he kept making succulent sounds with each sip of his black coffee, I thought it stunk and was glad when he finally put the lid on his thermos. Eventually, he pulled off to the side of the road, in a spot where empty plastic cups labeled "worms" and rusting beer and pop cans suggested other fishermen had stopped.

After parking, Mr. Rhinehart opened the trunk of the car and got out what he called his waders. They were nothing like the boots that Mama called galoshes, and made us wear during the winter. His boots went up to his hips, and had straps that he fastened onto his belt. While

I was studying his waders and watching his struggle to get his first foot down into one of them, Mr. Rhinehart asked, "Where're your wading boots?" Never having heard of such boots, and not wanting to risk embarrassment, I responded, "I didn't bring any. I'm just going to use my tennis shoes."

"He, he, he, he. Your tennis shoes, huh?"

I heard that same crazy laugh from earlier this morning, and this time, I knew he was laughing at me. I began to wonder about the wisdom of having gone fishing, miles away, in a wooded area, by myself, with this white man. Mama and Daddy let me go with Mr. Rhinehart because they knew he was the newspaper customer who gave me the biggest tips, and at Christmas time, he always gave me a bag of cookies and candy. During the summer, he allowed Daddy, my brothers, and me to pick buckets of apples from the trees in his yard. He was the only white man who had befriended me up to that point in my life, but it was unheard of for a white man to take, as we were called then, a Negro or colored child on a recreational trip. Yet it bothered me when he laughed at me, called me "Jackie," and said things such as, "Fish, fish in the brook, come and get on Jackie's hook."

It felt like he was talking down to me in the form of a nursery rhyme designed for a much younger child. I had heard a white nurse talk the same way to my mother while visiting our house. The nurse lived in Westmont, a white suburb of Johnstown, and although she was proud of being a college graduate, she still said to Mama, "Gracie, you no feel so good today. Me check you, and you be okay." In addition, with the fame of Willie Mays and Jackie Robinson, I had heard more than one white person call a Negro child "Willie" or "Jackie," regardless of their actual names. While he was working as a shoeshine boy in downtown Johnstown, I heard a white man say to my friend, Tyrone, "Hey, Jackie. How about a shine?" When my friends and I were selling peanuts, potato chips, and pop at Point Stadium baseball games, white adults sometimes got our attention with things such as, "Hey, Willie, over here!"

We gathered our fishing equipment, and before I could figure him out, we had walked down to the riverbank of the Little River. Mr. Rhinehart waded into the water, which came up over the knees of his boots. I stuck one foot into the cold water and jumped back as though I had been bitten. He started his "he, he, he," laughing, and this time it reminded me of how those beer-drinking white men in the cowboy movies sounded once they got drunk, started laughing, hollering, and shooting at another man's feet. It was a good thing that he didn't call me "Jackie" just then because I would have said to him, "My name is Jack." I would have said it in the same tone of voice Uncle Zack said he used when he came home from overseas during World War II, and a half-drunk white man asked, "Where are you shipping in from, boy?" Uncle Zack sobered him up by answering gruffly, "How big are the boys where you come from?"

Mr. Rhinehart headed downstream and slowly disappeared around the bend. Meanwhile, after making several perfect casts into likely spots for big fish, not even a nibble came my way. So, I just cast my bait straight out into the river, let the finishing nail carry it to the bottom, and put the rod on the ground. It seemed like an hour had passed, and I hadn't caught a thing. Sitting there, I began thinking about how my friends would tease me when I returned empty handed. They'd never understand that it wasn't my fault that Daddy might have dug up the wrong kind of worms, and whatever kind they were, the Crisco can might have left my worms with an odor that the fish couldn't stand. I considered the possibility that Mr. Rhinehart wasn't catching anything either, and as I wondered what he was doing, my line started moving slowly through the water. Jumping to my feet, I jerked the rod into the air, forgot to wind the reel, ran back a few steps, and dragged the fish up the bank. I had him!

Flopping on the ground was a huge—the largest I had ever seen— rainbow trout. After holding the fish down with my foot, along with a portion of its gills, I ripped the hook out of its mouth. When the fish stopped jumping and was breathing slightly with a trickle of blood coming through his mouth, I placed him in my Crisco can, on top of my bait. Then, in what seemed to be just a few minutes after I had cast out again, "bang," another big one hit. Soon, my Crisco can was full to the brim with rainbow trout, and I could hardly wait for Mr. Rhinehart to return.

As he waded toward me, he made what seemed to be ridiculous long casts across the river. He was winding the line in before a fish could possibly bite, and, to make matters worse, he didn't have a worm on his hook. Instead, he had some kind of metal object with two dangling, three-pronged hooks covered by thin strips of green and yellow green plastic. Maybe, he was just practicing, the way I had once seen his next-door neighbor practice with a plastic golf ball. When he was about five feet from me, he asked, "How'd you do Jackie?" Simultaneously, he lifted a chain out of the water, mentioning the names of two different kinds of bass, though I could see that they were the same kinds of fish I had seen on his grass. There were about six snaps on the chain, and, on each snap, there were one or two big fish. One was bigger and looked meaner than any of those I had seen in his yard; It seemed strange that he had caught anything since he clearly did not have any bait on the metal object with the yellow and green plastic strips.

Even though they were big, he only had more of those large, bronze colored fish, whereas I had caught several rainbow trout, the fish every fisherman sought. As he was coming out of the water, I tilted my Crisco can and said, "Look, I've got a bunch of rainbow trout." Again, he started that weird "he, he, he" laughing, and spit into the river, leaving drips of dark-brown tobacco juice on his stubby blond beard. "Rainbow trout, huh Jackie?" Then, he stumbled back into the water.

White people sure can be silly, I thought. Here he was, laughing crazily at me for no reason that I could determine, and he was the one who had just missed falling completely into the river. Since I didn't know why he was laughing at me, I assumed that it had something to do with my color—the way I knew some white people told jokes about colored people eating watermelons, stealing chickens, and being stupid in general. If I had had another way to get back home, I would have told him about that "Jackie" stuff right then and there, and run the risk of him leaving me.

Although I was dead tired on the return trip to Johnstown, I was kept awake by the prospect of showing off my big catch. Mr. Rhinehart had the radio station tuned to what seemed like a Lawrence Welk special. When that station faded, he switched to a station playing nothing but polkas. Occasionally, he sang along with the chorus of a song. I was glad that he was singing, and not asking me for the fourth time about the rainbow trout I had caught. About an hour later, he dropped me off in front of my house. I grabbed my rod and Crisco can, hopped out of the car with a "Thanks, Mr. Rhinehart," and raced into the house to show Mama and Daddy my fish. I hadn't taken three steps across the kitchen floor before Mama yelled, "Ooh Lawd have mercy! Boy get those things out of here!"

As I went into the backyard, I felt really great about the fact that Mama was afraid of my big fish and the one or two slimy worms that remained in my Crisco can. I was also glad that Mama didn't ask if I had eaten my apple, which, while fishing, I had thrown as far across the river as I could, and then watched drift out of sight. I felt even better when Daddy came out back and said, "Those sure are some nice 'chubbies.' I'm going to clean and eat every one of them."

After I laid my fish and rod out on the grass, the way that I had seen Mr. Rhinehart leave his fishing stuff in his yard, I went to tell all of my friends about my first fishing trip. None of them believed me. I thought to myself, "What do they know? There's a lot to know about fishing, and none of them have ever been fishing in their lives. What else can you expect from them?" As Daddy often said about such people, they were just ignorant. Besides, Mr. Rhinehart had invited me to go fishing again, and I eagerly looked forward to going with him. Maybe, I would catch more and bigger fish, and show them to all of my doubting friends.

Something very revealing took place on my next fishing trip with Mr. Rhinehart. Braving the cold water, I slid right into the river behind him. Right away, I noticed that he was using worms instead of metal and plastic objects. Before heading downstream, he cast a worm near where I had fished. He waited a minute or two, and I watched as, with a quick jerk, he set the hook and reeled in a rainbow trout, larger than any I had caught on my first trip with him. In disgust, he took the fish off the hook and hurled it across the river. I couldn't believe what he had done. Before I could ask him about throwing away such a big fish, he said, "Damn chubbie stole my bait. I'd better tie on one of my spinners and move on down the river."

As the name "chubbie" sank deep into my mind along with the fact that the thrown away fish was quite large, my heart began to sink with the possibility of my fish having been something other than rainbow trout. That terrible possibility was strengthened by my memory of Daddy having also said something about chubbies. All day, I wondered and worried each time that I added a rainbow trout to my can. As I stood in the place where the fish were biting, Mr. Rhinehart gradually waded out of my sight. Near noon, he returned with his usual stringer of fish, only this time he also had two pretty multicolored fish. Taken by their size, shape and color, I inquired, "What kind are those two with all of the colors?"

"They're sunfish, really good eating. They have colors like those chubbies you've been catching, but they are much better eating. Fishermen don't fish for chubbies because they will hit at any darn thing you toss out there, and besides, chubbies have so many fine bones that you can't eat them."

I didn't care what Mr. Rhinehart had to say about chubbies. I loved their beautiful colors and the fact that the chubbies constantly attacked your bait, giving plenty of action. Their quick "tap, tap, tap" was simply a big hungry fish that was about to grab my bait. I spent hours standing in the same spot, fishing for chubbies, and I kept every one that I caught. Instead of continuing to use my Crisco can to hold them, I made a fish stringer by tying together two long shoelaces from Daddy's old work shoes. To stop the chubbies from sliding off my stringer, I found a six- or seven-inch bolt in Mr. Grey's junkyard, took it home, and tied it to one end of the shoelaces. To help guide the shoelaces through the gills of the fish, I tied a large nail at the other end. I felt so proud when I returned home, and held up my shoestring of chubbies for Daddy and Mama to see.

Since Mama and Daddy had been cooking and eating my fish, I thought Mr. Rhinehart's chubbie comments amounted to another instance of white people not knowing what they were talking about, just like my white school friends didn't know anything about eating delicious collard greens. However, when I bit into my first piece of a chubbie, I was reminded of eating cotton candy with all of its fine strands—only these fine strands got caught in my throat instead of gently melting. At first, it felt as though there were a lot of little things scratching my throat, and to "wash it down," I took a bite from one of Mama's homemade rolls. Because of the urge to remove the feeling in my throat, I didn't chew it well and the bread got stuck. I jumped up, gasping for air. Seeing that I needed help, Mama came toward me shouting, "Lawd have mercy! What's wrong with you boy?"

I pointed to my throat, and Mama started slapping me on my back. As she held my one hand over my head and continued to slap me, I was reminded of my past whippings by her. Finally, I coughed up the bread and bones, and after I got my breath, I began to wipe tears from my eyes. My taste for chubbies was gone.

The next time that I went fishing with Mr. Rhinehart, I brought along an extra pair of pants. The last irritating ride home in wet pants had done it for me, and now I would change at the end of the day, the way he always did, even though his waders had prevented him from getting wet. I also listened attentively to everything he told me about fishing, including the fact that fishermen didn't fish for chubbies. Instead of staying in a spot where the chubbies hit, I started following Mr. Rhinehart down the river, always moving when he moved and remaining about fifteen or so yards behind him, watching carefully everything that he did. Eventually I turned the bend where he had previously disappeared from my view as I remained behind fishing for chubbies. After watching him catch several fish from one spot and move on, I waded as close as I could to the place he had just left.

The water gradually deepened, preventing me from reaching exactly where Mr. Rhinehart had stood. However, I could see a submerged, shadowy object, and I cast toward it. My bait landed in front of the object, and within minutes, I had hooked my first rock bass, added the fish to my shoelace stringer, and tied it to my belt. After I had caught three more rock bass, I noticed that Mr. Rhinehart was on the move again, and so I left my spot.

Wading slowly toward Mr. Rhinehart, I looked at my four rock bass, and it occurred to me that I didn't catch a single chubbie in the spot I had just left. When I got closer to Mr. Rhinehart, I noticed that he was casting one of his metal lures quite a distance into some fast-running water. As I hung back and watched what he was doing, I saw him repeatedly make casts and slowly retrieve. On about the seventh cast, his rod tip took a big dip, he jerked upwards, and I saw a big smallmouth bass come up out of the water. I watched everything he did as he fought the fish, eventually lifted a small net from his side, and scooped up the fish. After he snapped the fish on his metal stringer, Mr. Rhinehart started wading to another spot, all the time casting and slowly retrieving.

I carefully made my way near the place where he had caught the smallmouth bass, but once again the water was too deep for me, and I was unable to cast my worm far enough to reach the fast water. After several failed attempts, I reached into my pants pocket, pulled out three more finishing nails, and tied them to my line. Then, I stripped some line off my reel, and making a two-handed cast, hurled the finishing nails and worm into the fast water. Since the nails took my bait near the place where Mr. Rhinehart' big fish first came out of the water, I didn't move the bait. While waiting for something to happen, it occurred to me that Mr. Rhinehart always wound his lure back, but I was unable to do that with the reel he had sold me.

My reel was the kind that I saw fishermen use to cast dry flies. Whereas they would make several whip-like motions, back and forth over their heads, and then cast their flies a long distance, I had to strip some line off the reel, and then sling my bait as far as the weight of one finishing nail sinker and a nightcrawler would go. Because my small reel handle was not strong enough to wind in a fish once it was hooked, I had to pull the line with my left hand, then wind up the slack, and repeat this pattern until the fish was close enough to be grabbed. But Mr. Rhinehart had some kind of reel with which he could easily make long casts and retrieves. Winding his reel, he eventually got his fish close enough to dip them up with a small net he had fastened to his belt. And so, not having all of that fancy equipment, and having gotten my bait over into the fast water anyway, I just let it sit.

After keeping a close eye on my line for what seemed like an endless time, I got a "tap, tap, tap," and then my line began to move quickly. I jerked upward on my rod, the same way I saw Mr. Rhinehart hook his fish. There was a considerable struggle as the fish swam against the fast current, and the weight of the four finishing nails put added tension on my line. Once I got it out of the fast water, the fish came slowly toward me, and eventually I had in my hand the largest chubbie I had ever seen. With my chest pounding, I quickly added him to my four rock bass, and headed in the direction of Mr. Rhinehart.

I followed all day, far enough behind him to stay out of his way, but close enough to figure out things he was doing. One time I saw him switch to a worm, cast near the bank, catch two small sunfish, release them, and move on. It was a real sense of accomplishment when I got to that spot and began to catch sunfish. Indeed, I learned a lot that day because, that evening, as I followed Mr. Rhinehart up the bank toward the car, I had my largest catch ever—eight rock bass, four sunfish, and one huge chubbie.

Thinking about what had happened as I followed, watched, and copied Mr. Rhinehart, I realized that rock bass liked to hang out in deep water that contained some sort of object, while smallmouth bass preferred fast current. My four sunfish were caught in shallow water near the bank, and, because of their small mouths, it was easier to catch them by using only half a worm. Walking back, I looked at Mr. Rhinehart' five or six big smallmouth bass, and then I noticed that he had more and bigger rock bass than I had caught. That's when I decided that I needed to find out more about the reel and lure that he used. When he got back to the car and sat his rod down to take off his boots, I sat down by his equipment and took a close look at his reel and lure. On his reel, there was some clear line, and my reel had thicker line that looked more like string.

As soon as he started driving, I asked, "What kind of line is that you have on your reel, and what kind of lure is that?" After turning down the radio and then spitting tobacco juice out of his window, he answered, "Jackie, I use a spinning reel with monofilament line, and I use it to cast a Green Devil. Yes sir, that Green Devil sure wakes up those big small-mouth bass." Then came that familiar "he, he, he" laugh of his. This time, I didn't think he was laughing at me because the next thing he said was, "Don't you worry, Jackie. You're going to be some kind of fisherman. Yes sir, I'll tell you. That's a nice mess of fish you have on that stringer of yours."

Over the next couple of trips, I worried less and less about Mr. Rhinehart, his use of "Jackie," and that laugh of his; I guess I came to believe that they weren't personal. Plus, I needed to think about where the different kinds of fish liked to hang out and what it took to catch them, and I wanted to watch Mr. Rhinehart as much as I could in order to learn more about fishing. So I always followed him, doing whatever I saw him do as best I could with my equipment. Each trip, I caught a few more fish and they were a little larger. At the same time, Mr. Rhinehart did things that caused me to think that he had grown to like me more than when we first started fishing together.

During one trip, my can of pop got too hot to drink as it sat in the backseat of his car. On the very next trip, Mr. Rhinehart brought for me several cans of pop in his blue ice chest where he also kept two or three bottles of beer. On the ride home, instead of napping and trying to ignore the polkas playing on the radio, I'd talk to Mr. Rinehart about the day's fishing. To make sure that I hadn't just been lucky and to see if there was something else I needed to know, I began to tell him about the best spots and kinds of water for catching different kinds of fish. Sometimes he would say, "Yeah, but . . . ," and then add something about water temperatures, depth, color, or flow in relation to what I had said. More and more, I knew that I was on the right track because increasingly he just said, "That's right, Jackie." By August, our fishing trips ended routinely with, "When are we going again, Jackie?"

"Whenever you want to go!"

Regardless of Mr. Rhinehart's beliefs or motives, he presented the chance to engage in something for which I had a passionate desire. Yet, over the years, he became a haunting force in my life, periodically causing me to become extremely conflicted. Because I valued so highly the positive fishing experiences he afforded me, I didn't want to acknowledge those things that left me viewing him in a negative fashion. Seeking psychological refuge, I tried to turn his shortcomings into virtues. No, he didn't give me the fishing equipment or the instructions I needed. Because he did not simply spoon-feed me, I learned to solve problems for myself, to be thrifty and save, and to make the best of a great opportunity. Had he provided a handout, such as a pair of wading boots, I wouldn't have experienced the joy of purchasing my own boots that very next summer, after dutifully saving for months. Surviving his trial by fire, I gained considerable self-confidence with regard to wading the river, confidence that later carried over to resolving other difficult circumstances.

Slowly and painfully, though, there was no denying that he took me fishing, but he didn't teach me to fish. Mr. Rhinehart provided a tremendous opportunity, but he didn't show me how to take full advantage. Instead, I had to figure things out for myself, to experience the cold water while wading in tennis shoes and the discomfort of riding home in wet pants before I learned to bring a second pair of pants to change into for the ride home. Necessity, not Mr. Rhinehart, taught me.

The more I learned about the reel he sold me, the more I felt like a fool. When that initially fascinating burgundy metal began to rust and the gold swirls chipped after just two fishing trips, I felt so stupid to once have thought the reel was coated with precious metals. The more insights I gained about fishing and Mr. Rhinehart, the more disappointed I became with him. He sold a naive child a reel that was used by advanced fishermen to cast dry flies, not by a beginner to toss concocted sinkers and earthworms. With that reel, I could not cast lures and retrieve them as he did with his spinning reel, the equipment he preferred for the kind of fishing he did. The memory of a wonderful reel, sold by a righteous person for a modest price, became tarnished by the thought of an opportunist selling me something he wanted to get rid of, a piece of junk. And my negative feelings toward him grew as I continued to savor the fun I had fishing with him.

I tried to cling to my savior, my fishing benefactor, but it grew increasingly difficult to do so. It was impossible to dismiss the fact that even as I waded in his shadows, never once did he caution me about the possibilities of a sudden drop-off in the river. I first learned about dangerous water depths the time I stepped into water over my shoulders. My bait floated out of my Crisco can, and momentarily I was terrified, struggling toward more shallow water. It is still hard for me to believe that Mr. Rinehart didn't gain some perverse satisfaction when he laughed and inquired sarcastically, "Are you taking a bath, Jackie?" And shouldn't he have shared his seldom-used worms with me after I struggled to the bank, climbed out of the river, and sat there drying in the sun, unable to fish?

I still wonder if some of Mr. Rinehart's "he, he, he" laughs were mocking my shoelace fish stringer. Why didn't he ever let me use one of his stringers, one of those extra metal chains he always had in his car? Daddy at least made me a bait can, showed me how to dig for bait, and gave me money to buy hooks and line. In addition, Daddy never laughed at my chubbies; he encouraged me by eating them.

With Mr. Rinehart as my only salvation, "Jackie" became something I shamefully endured. "Jackie" was also a name my male peers used to tease me, a name signifying that my masculinity was being called into question. They knew that taunting me with "Jackie" could easily lead to a fistfight, so much so that I once fought a losing battle with Johnnie Suggs, even though he was three years older and much bigger. Had one of my friends heard Mr. Rinehart call me "Jackie," there would have been endless ridicule. Carrying this secret tolerance of Mr. Rhinehart, it seemed to become more sordid with time, refusing to release me even as I approached adulthood.

During my early college days, I was growing in my racial conscious-ness, and there was no way I could tell my "black power" college friends about my white fishing friend. At that time, the circulating white male demonology held that "the white man" was the source of all of "the black man's" troubles. I was supposed to hate "the white man" for his part in the horrors of the middle passage, lynchings in America, and seg-regation throughout the country. Because I thought about the possibility that I had been a "house Negro" who had "gone along to get along" with the "master," a pervasive sense of guilt accompanied my reflections on those joyful days of fishing with Mr. Rhinehart. Even the "Mr. Rhine-hart" bit began to eat away at my self-esteem. Although as a child I called adults "Mr." or "Miss" or "Mrs.," now it seemed "Uncle Tommish" to still, in college, call him "Mr. Rhinehart." Even more frustrating was the possibility that I had adopted the "Uncle Tom" persona so well that I knew nothing else to call him. A prisoner to my upbringing, anything other than "Mr." was not a permissible reality for me, and so I never learned his first name.

I never thought the day would come when I would not find fault with the fact that Uncle Tom loved his master, savored the material advan-tages, and cherished the other opportunities he provided. However, Mr. Rhinehart helped me revisit my understanding of that iconoclastic figure. Like Uncle Tom, at the time that I fished with Mr. Rhinehart, my uni-verse was limited to what my "master" permitted me to experience and others failed to provide. Unfortunately, Uncle Tom never gained access to the kind of liberating experiences I received as I fished with other African American men, experiences that enabled me to put Mr. Rhine-hart into proper and, finally, peaceful perspective.

As best I could, I finally put Mr. Rhinehart in safe mental storage, telling myself that he gave me what he could. And, most importantly, he wasn't my father. He wasn't the one with whom I wanted a less work, less

God, more fun relationship. Although he helped me get bait and other fishing supplies, I felt let down by Daddy, who was always too busy working to take me fishing. When he wasn't working, he was too busy assigning jobs for me to do or helping me to find God, both of which were to keep me out of trouble. He never seemed to realize that I wanted the comfort of his company as much as he thought I needed the comfort of God. Mr. Rhinehart wasn't the one from whom I wanted the reassurance of being taught how to avoid painful mistakes, rather than having to learn so many things by trial and error. Not until he was an old man, retired from years of strenuous, debilitating, manual labor, did I get a chance to fish with Daddy. And then I was sorry that it had taken so long to experience the father-son intimacy that flowed from those experiences, an intimacy that is also needed by so many young African American males who accept the first "Mr. Rhinehart" who enters their lives.

5

THE BIG RIVER

DEACON ARMSTRONG, my younger brother Stephen's godfather, didn't laugh or say much to me other than, "Son, listen to what God is trying to tell you." One day, while he was visiting my parents, my father got him talking when he said, "Come over here son, and tell Deacon Armstrong about those fish you caught with Rhinehart. Deacon Armstrong, this boy is a real fisherman." Deacon Armstrong listened pa tiently to my description of how I caught the first chubbies, all the others, the sunfish, and rock bass I had caught since, and then said, "If you think it's good fishing over in the little river, just wait until I get you up to the big river. I'll show you how to catch some bass bigger than my arm." He was a huge, muscular man from working in the coal mines, and looking at his well-formed arms, I asked, "Bigger than your arms?"

"Yes, indeed. Son, you know those little fish you caught over in the little river? Well up on the big river we use them for bait. You just listen to what God is trying to tell you, and one day I might take you fishing there. You'll see."

"When you get one that big, how do you get him out of the water and onto your stringer?"

"I carry a lead billy club wrapped in a leather pouch. As soon as I lift one of those big boogers into the boat, I knock it in the head, right behind the eyes, and that stops all that jumping around."

I had my doubts about the things Deacon Armstrong bragged about having done on that big river of his, but I dismissed them. After all, he was a deacon; everybody knew that God "called" deacons right after he finished "calling" ministers, and so I figured he couldn't be lying. Besides, Daddy sat there smiling, as if everything Deacon Armstrong told us was the gospel truth. I couldn't wait to see just how big that river and those fish really were.

Thereafter, every time I saw Deacon Armstrong, he would indicate that he would take me fishing with him one day; the "one day" part reminded me of Uncle Youngie's promise to take me fishing "one day" on the James River, so I sat as close as possible to the "Deacons' bench" in church, hoping that Deacon Armstrong noticed how well I was listening to what God was trying to tell me. I often thought about not having taken Jesus as my personal savior, and I wondered whether that was why Deacon Armstrong hadn't invited me to go fishing. Believing in that possibility, I kept looking for an opportunity to impress him with my spiritual salvation.

One humid Sunday morning before the preacher stood up in the pulpit, the deacons had "warmed things up" with "Jesus, the Light of the World," and then had gotten half of the congregation spiritually "happy" by singing a very emotional version of "Come to Jesus." You needed a heart of granite not to have been moved by their pleading, emotional rendition of the song. Not wanting to miss a chance, like the night I fell asleep during the revival service in Virginia, I sang along enthusiastically, "Come to Jesus, come to Jesus, right now, right now." This Sunday, I would let neither Jesus nor Deacon Armstrong's promise slip away.

I hoped my vigorous singing indicated that I had accepted Jesus as my personal savior, and that I was "listening to what God was trying to tell me." Later, as Reverend Jefferson preached about Jesus having "all power in his hands," I nodded my head in agreement each time Daddy said something like "Yes, Lord" or "Teach them, Reverend." Once, when

Deacon Armstrong gave the minister a hardy "Amen, go on and preach Rev," I said a robust, seemingly spontaneous, "Amen." Mrs. Womack heard me, and the flickering possibility of God having touched a child got the spirit moving in her. "Help that child, Lord," she said, waving her handkerchief in a frantic motion and starting a rhythmic stomping of her feet. I started clapping my hands in time with her stomping feet, and she screamed, "Suffer the little children! God's working in here today." And when Daddy gave a sign of approval by smiling at me, I stood up along with about ten other people who were clapping, waving their hands, and hollering as Reverend Jefferson was screaming, "All power, all power, not government power, not green power, but JeeeeeSuss has all power in his hands." By the time that we sat down, my hands were red and stinging.

It seemed as though that church service would last forever, and I was sorry that I had helped to encourage Reverend Jefferson. He got so caught up in his emotional singsong sermon and the congregation's responses that he realized neither how hot it was nor that the ushers had already given smelling salts to two people and carried them out of the church. He just continued whooping and hollering about the power of "a mighty Jesus" until he finally became hoarse and had to quit preaching. The choir took up where he left off, and pushed on with no mercy as they sang for sinners to come forward and accept the Lord Jesus as their personal savior. Despite my, the old saints', and the choir's best efforts, no one came forward to join the church, and, at the end of the service, Deacon Armstrong said nothing to me about fishing.

The next Sunday, I just sat in church and waited for God to tell me something. Nothing at all spiritual happened to me during the service, and as I was leaving, I was thinking about playing in a pickup football game with my friends later that evening. Everyone was shaking hands and giving "Christian hugs and kisses" when suddenly one of Deacon Armstrong's coarse coal mining hands engulfed one of mine, and he said, "Son, you want to go fishing with me up on the big river?" I yelled excitedly, "Yes sir! Thank you, Jesus!"

Deacon Armstrong blew his horn in front of the house right at five o'clock the next Friday. After I put my things in the back and hopped into the front seat, Mama yelled from the porch, "Deacon Armstrong, you take care of my son. Don't let him drown up there on that river. They said that Mr. Littlejohn's nephew fell in up there, and it took three of them to pull him out. You make sure you get my boy back before it's too late Saturday night because Sunday is the first Sunday, and Jack Lee has to help wash the communion glasses." Deacon Armstrong offered a polite, "Okay, Sis Daniel, he'll be safe with me. You know I won't let anything happen to your boy," and then gradually pulled away from the curb.

We hadn't gone two blocks before he said, "You heard your mother. When we get to the river, you do as I tell you. There are some deep holes up there, and you don't go wading anywhere I don't tell you to go." Appreciating the advice, I replied, "Yes sir. I'll be right by your side."

I daydreamed in the cab of Deacon Armstrong's old, dented, black pickup truck as we chugged along for more than two hours through the rural Pennsylvania mountains, shifting gears, and occasionally drifting to the side of the road to let cars pass while we labored up hills. Soon we crossed the Huntingdon bridge, and for the first time, I saw the main branch of the Juniata. It was deeper and wider than anything I had expected, but I was confident that I could handle whatever awaited me in that big, bad river.

In a short while, we left the pavement and went about ten miles along a winding, one-lane dirt road. Just past a big cornfield that stretched so far it met the sky, I got my first glimpse of his two-room cabin, situated about thirty yards from a big bend in the river. I felt like a real frontiersman as I studied the old, dark brown, weather worn, wooden-framed building with its stone chimney. I was ready to go fishing, to test the big river, but I had to wait until some work was completed.

Deacon Armstrong had decided to restock his cabin supplies, and so he had all kinds of extra stuff in the back of the truck; in addition to garden tools and three large bags of fertilizer, he had a lawn mower, a case of red beans, two sacks of rice, a slab of bacon, several bags of sugar (which he loved to pour into black coffee), five one-gallon jugs of drinking water, and a case of ginger ale which he claimed was "good for your stomach." Unloading the truck seemed interminable, and each passing minute seemed to let another big fish get away. Finally, finished with the unloading, he went to check on his garden while I remained in the cabin, fascinated by the variety of guns and rods along the walls. Soon, I would get a chance to see what Deacon Armstrong could do with the rod he called "Old Betsy," with its fifteen-pound test line.

As the sun started to fade, he began to load rods, nets, bait, and his blackjack into the boat. I thought, "Gee, he wasn't lying about that blackjack." In addition to worms, he also had, wrapped in a rag, some funny smelling stuff which he called "dough bait." I asked,

"How did you make that stuff?"

"Before we go fishing again, you come over to my house, and I'll show you."

"Worms have been working for me. Why do I need that stuff?"

"Worms are fine for rock bass and bluegills, but you need some of this dough bait for those big cats on the bottom of the river. With dough bait, you can get a hold of some cats almost as big as you. That's why I put that extra rod in the boat, just in case they start biting and you needed a rod with some fifteen-pound test instead of that rod and reel of yours."

This, I had to see. For this trip, my bait can consisted of a big pork and beans can on which I had left the lid partially attached when I opened it, so I could pull it down to keep the sun off my worms. As he paddled upstream, I looked at my worms and fantasized that I caught more and bigger fish than he did with his dough bait. My daydreaming was interrupted by, "Drop the anchor. This is one of those deep holes where those arm's length bass like to feed at night. See that big tree hanging over the water; it will help you find this deep hole again."

Both the "deep hole" and the prospects of "arm's length" bass had me almost shaking with anticipation, but that part about all of this happening "at night" struck a different nerve. Seeing that blackjack on the floor of the boat didn't help much either; just how big did a fish have to be if it needed to be knocked out once it was in the boat? Not wanting to appear fearful, I simply asked, "Deacon Armstrong, why did you wait so late to come out here?" In a matter-of-fact tone, he replied, "Because that's when the big fish start feeding. During the day, you catch more of those little fish you caught in the little river."

A silent, thick, dark night came much sooner than I preferred, but vicious mosquitoes kept me from worrying too much. They found every exposed part of my body, and some even bit through my shirt. Not being able to see where to cast, and needing a free hand to swat mosquitoes, I just dropped my line straight down and waited. I don't remember how long it took but the hole had to be very deep given the amount of line that came off my reel before the bait hit the bottom of the river. Then I waited, and waited, and waited some more, while listening to what sounded like a million insects singing in the woods.

Suddenly, without saying a word, and with much determination, Deacon Armstrong gave a strong, upward, rod-bending jerk. A few minutes later, the fifteen-pound test line had served its purpose, and for a few seconds something was thumping around in the boat. Then there was a thud, like a boxer hitting a punching bag, and, simultaneously, what sounded like a tree branch cracking; Deacon Armstrong had used his blackjack to crack the fish's skull. The flopping stopped. He dropped the fish into a netted sack, tied the sack to the boat, tossed the sack into the water, wiped his bloody hand on his pants, and broke the silence. "What did I tell you son? Now you know that there are some big boogers in this river. Now, do you want to try some of this dough bait?" Full of foolish teenage pride, I answered, "No sir, these worms work, too."

The night stood still as I waited for one of those big boogers to hit my line, and it got darker and darker as I waited. Using his dough bait, which he mashed like a big wad of bubble gum around his hook, Deacon Armstrong caught two more giant catfish with big, sagging, yellow bellies. Meanwhile, my nail and worm just sat on the bottom of the river, and I was very happy when Deacon Armstrong finally said, "Pull the anchor."

I tried to comply, but it seemed to be stuck on the muddy river bottom. Before I could get it to budge, in a desperate sounding voice, he repeated, "Pull the anchor!" Again, I was unable to move the anchor, but the boat started turning slowly and we began moving gradually upstream as Deacon Armstrong held his bent rod with two hands. I didn't remember having seen or heard a motor on the boat, yet we were definitely moving upstream. For much too long, Deacon Armstrong didn't speak, and although I listened and wanted either him or God to speak, neither he nor God told me anything.

Deacon Armstrong kept maneuvering whatever was on the end of the line, and I kept trying to follow his rowing instructions; gradually, we got the boat to the bank. Before I could refuse to accept his fishing rod, he handed it to me, jumped out, and began tying the boat to a tree. I felt as though I was in a horror movie when he said, "Okay son, you hold him while I go back to the house to get the clamps. I have some clamps that I can slide down the line and sink into his jaws. Just hold him, and I will be right back." I thought, "Clamps? Clamps?"

My imagination began racing wildly out of control as I wondered what could possibly be down there that needed clamps through its jaws. What if it came to the surface and looked me in the face? Then what would I do? Did Deacon Armstrong really believe that I was going to sit there in the dark, holding onto who knew what, while he walked to the cabin and back? Sure, I might have been a little crazy to have been out there at night with him in the first place, but as we always said at home, I was no fool.

Before Deacon Armstrong could leave, and just as I decided that land was the best place for me, whatever had come out of that deep hole began a strong, steady, unyielding movement toward the deepest part of the river. Its diving motion lifted me out of my seat, and I placed one foot on the top of the boat's side, preparing to jump. Noting my distress, Deacon Armstrong nearly knocked me down as he got back in the boat, grabbed the rod from me, and held on as line streamed off the reel. Suddenly there was a loud sound similar to a gunshot, followed by "God-damn that booger. Hot damn! Hot damn! That son of a gun ran like a bat out of hell, and snapped my best damn line. Come on boy, let's go. With all the ruckus that booger just made, we ain't gonna get nothing else out of that damn hole tonight."

I loved every moment of his frustration, especially the cursing. His almighty, goddamn, extra strong, fifteen-pound test line had been snapped! Never before and never since have I been as happy to see the "big one" get away. It was a truly great feeling to quit fishing that night. As we sat in silence, drifting downstream, my satisfaction blurred a bit with the realization that none of my closest pals were going to believe this—not even my best friend George. I could just hear myself pleading with him in frustration, "Honest man, whatever it was, it pulled me, Deacon Armstrong, the boat, and the anchor upstream! Man, it snapped his fifteen-pound test line. If I'm lying, I'm flying."

That night, approaching sleep with alternating thoughts of what might have been at the end of Deacon Armstrong's line and how I could possibly convince my friends of what had happened, I was sure of one thing: I was hooked on the possibilities of the big river, and whether they believed me or not, I couldn't wait to tell my friends about the trip.

The Carp

Looking back through old pictures
seeing myself holding the carp
remembering but unable to recall
his weight on the line
the length of the fight, my fatigue
or the joy of landing him.

I was too young to remember the story
so I must sit silent while the old men
tell their carp stories around the night fire

watch their age stand still
as they relive their battles.

It wasn't until this past summer
that I got another chance to battle the carp
I remember the strike, my rod doubled over
as he began to run down the river.
Glancing at my father
I saw him give me an encouraging smile
and I knew it was the carp that had come again.
The old men in the camp
heard the familiar screaming of the line
and journeyed down to watch the battle.

Each man stood silent,
critiquing my performance. I fought hard
keeping my poise like a good prizefighter.
The battle wore on, and as my muscles began to knot,
each of the old men began to leave their bodies.
They were going off to relive
their battles with the carp.
As each face began to look younger,
I knew that this carp would be mine.

The carp finally showed me his long yellow belly,
and I knew that he was tired
I pumped the fish, using all of my weight against him
He came toward me and our eyes met.
Then having known me, he closed his eyes
and I put my hand through his gills.
I lifted him up
out of the Juniata to show the old men,
but only saw the backs of their figures floating by.

On the second trip, as I was anticipating another night on his boat, he surprised me with, "Tomorrow morning, I'm going to take you somewhere you can use those worms of yours to catch some nice rock bass. You might even catch hold of a big black bass."

"Why do we have to wait until tomorrow? Which way is it?"

"Where I'm taking you, the fish feed early in the morning, on the shady side of the river before the sun comes up. You'll see in the morning."

Shortly after six o'clock in the morning, Deacon Armstrong awakened me and said, "Come on. I've got the truck loaded." I jumped into my clothing, and quickly got my gear into the truck. He drove about two miles up the river and pulled off into the weeds, just far enough off the road to allow other cars to pass. From my seat, I could see that the river was dotted with partially submerged large rocks, and a little stream emptying into the river caused the water to flow a little faster. Before I got out, he instructed, "See that little stream? It washes bait into the river. The rock bass wait behind those big rocks and grab the bait when it floats by. Right after that fast water curls around that biggest rock is where the black bass hang out. You cast all around those rocks and see what happens."

Now that he had made me a believer, I immediately said, "Okay. As soon as I get my stuff, I'm going right over there to that big rock near where the stream is emptying into the river." However, before I could move, Deacon Armstrong advised, "Wait a minute. Don't go too much further down that side of the river. There are some drop offs once you get below these rocks." With that, we got out and began to assemble our gear. When I picked up my rod and reel, he said, "Here, take this. You can't do much good with your rod and reel. And take this bag of lead shots to snap on your line for weights instead of those nails. I'll be over there with you in a minute."

Deacon Armstrong put into my hands the first spinning reel and rod I had ever used. The tiny lead split shots were easy to snap on, and suddenly I was making longer and more precise casts. For about half an hour, I cast as long and accurately as I could, almost forgetting about catching fish. As he predicted, I caught a number of huge rock bass, all bigger than any I had caught in the little river. The biggest catch of all came when Deacon Armstrong said, "Let's go. We have enough fish. And since you seem to like that rod and reel so much, they're yours." I must have startled him when I yelled, "Thaaank you!"

For years to come, fishing with other men, I only used the rod and reel Deacon Armstrong had given me. While using them, I often wished I had gotten the opportunity to learn more from him.

Fishing with Deacon Armstrong made me want to never return to the little river. I wanted to become the fisherman that he was, but his losing bout with black lung disease prevented me from fishing again with him.

A summer later, I really made it to the big time. Unable to go with Deacon Armstrong and not wanting to fish the little river again with Mr. Rhinehart, I finally got Daddy to convince Mama it was okay for me to go fishing on the big river with Uncle William and Uncle Nash. Two of the most popular men with women, men, and children throughout Johnstown, they cursed, told stories about the sexy women they had been with, and did what we called "talk a lot of shit." They drank their whiskey straight out of the bottle. They were such dynamic characters that I knew I was going to have fun, regardless of whether I caught any fish.

The first time they picked me up, they were running late. Uncle William had been in a high-stakes poker game all night, and Uncle Nash said he'd had trouble finding him. I had been sitting on the doorstep waiting for what seemed to be hours, but probably was only about twenty minutes. As soon as I saw their red and black Oldsmobile, I rushed to meet them. I hurriedly tossed my things into the trunk, and then hopped into the backseat. As the car pulled off, Uncle William said, "Nash, reach under the seat and get me that bottle so I can take a little hit for the road." Uncle Nash complained, "God damn Bill, you already drank most of this pint. Save me a little swallow. Shit!" Then Uncle William took a swallow that made a gurgling sound, and to indicate his appreciation for fine liquor, he exclaimed, "Myyyyyy Lord!" The alcohol's aroma filled the car, and I noticed that the drink seemed to do for Uncle William what hot black coffee did for Mr. Rhinehart when he took a sip from his green thermos on the way to the little river.

We got to the big river much faster than Deacon Armstrong had in his truck, and soon I was headed to the river with my gear stuffed into my pockets and my bait can strung across my shoulder. My uncles decided to have another drink, and they were still sipping whiskey, talking, and putting on their fishing clothing when my first cast was met by a hard-hitting fish that I had on my stringer in a few minutes. When I caught a beautiful, rainbow-colored chubbie and quickly released it, they smiled approvingly, and I knew that they knew that I could handle the big river. For about an hour or so, the three of us caught fish after fish, let some go, kept some, and enjoyed each other as much as the fishing. Throughout that day, my uncles seemed to be quite proud of me, and I basked in the warmth of their smiles. This was the beginning of countless satisfying weekends spent fishing with my uncles, enjoying their souls.

Friday and Saturday nights found them savoring their favorite camp dinner of fried potatoes with onions and green peppers; a mixed salad of onions, cucumbers, lettuce, tomatoes, and several dashes of brown vinegar, served in an aluminum pot substituting for a salad bowl; golden brown fried fish; and plenty of ice-cold beers and colas. "After-dinner drinks" consisted of shots of gin and vodka poured generously into paper cups. As they ate and drank into the night, we might hear Uncle William retell the story of the time that he caught a record-sized brown trout, noted that it was full of eggs, and gently returned it to the river. He never failed to get a rise out of us when, at the end of the story, having indicated that he kissed the fish on its mouth, he would say in a voice as if he were talking sexually to a woman, "Honey, you a little too far gone for me to mess with you. I'll have to let you go, but I'll be back to take care of your babies." Deeper into the night, as one by one we went to bed, those half asleep would be awakened by the sounds of spinning tires and gravel flying. Uncle Nash would have finished his drink, gotten into his car, and sped off across town to the Elks club. Then, the bus's residents slipped into their dreams.

Becoming Part of Her

The creek trickled into the Juniata,
—a continuous mating ritual—
though the Juniata was far larger,
she took special care with him
taking him into her bosom
warming him, then making him
part of her.

The Juniata, like a mature woman, knows
what a young male needs. She makes his
first time soft,
warming him against her,
taking special care
not to just take him
into her.

It has been many years since
I have felt that special warmth.
In my first sexual experience
I was made part of her.
I remember seeing her through the
just pinkening apple blossoms.
She was placid and calm.
I walked out into the Juniata,
the algae on the pebbles tickled my feet.
I went into the water up to my neck.
She would rock me up onto my toes,
then subside, settling me back on my heels.
The water touched my lips and it was sweet.
The next wave swept me off of my toes,
my nails gently scraped a stone as my body
was carried off into her current.

I felt her tuck me into her,
and carry me off, a strange

warmth, as we sped up,
brought my senses alive, I could hear
a bluegill mashing a worm in his flat teeth,
and a catfish's antenna rubbing along
the bottom of the river. She turned me over
and I saw the sky filtered through her eyes

As was increasingly the case when I reflected on my son's poetry, memories, experiences and emotions long ignored or unrecognized surfaced from within me, as though finally having found their proper context. In this instance, I recalled a girl from my past. As soon as her name reemerged, I wondered why, until that moment, I had never associated the Juniata with Juanita, a girl I worshipped through high school. Pushing back my usual impulse to avoid too much emotional territory and its meaning, I began to explore what was in my head about Juanita, and to do so without, as Jerri put it to me, "trying to remain intellectual about someone you once adored." I thought I had disposed of the high-school experience by clinging to the thought that my years of successful marriage had cured me of whatever I once felt for Juanita. Now, Omari's poem triggered my high-school emotions and they bubbled to the surface of my consciousness, causing me to wonder what would have happened had I become part of her.

I hadn't seen her since we graduated from high school in June 1960. Yet, more than thirty years later, I still remembered her as the most intelligent and pretty girl I knew in high school. Juanita had smooth, unblemished, dark-chocolate skin. She was short and had what seemed to be softball-sized breasts, a perfectly formed waist, and a butt that looked like the perfect curve of a question mark. She also had the sexiest bowed legs I had ever seen.

I remembered how I felt the time I got to hold her on first base. While she stood near the base and I stood a step or two to the right and behind her, I could see her Vaseline-oiled arms and legs emerging from her powder blue shorts and white blouse. I was four or five inches taller, and, after she had hit the ball and run to first, I was able to look down and admire the way her lovely breasts rose and sank with each breath she took. As I held her close to the base, I prayed that no one would get a hit, sending her off to second. When my pitcher threw over to first, I put a long tag right on her butt.

When the batter hit a pop fly out near second base, Juanita started running, but stopped and began to retreat when the second baseman caught the fly ball and threw it to me. After it popped in my glove, I tried to avoid tagging her, but she ran right into me. In typical adolescent turmoil, I was glad to end the inning, sorry about putting her out, but thrilled by the opportunity to be so close to her again.

We were close friends throughout high school, but I never made it with Juanita. When she teased me, gently hitting her was as close as I came to touching her. When we had chances to talk, her presence became too large for me. My throat got dry, my tongue became immobile, and I could never "drop my lines." I was great when it came to dropping lines on girls for whom the *act* of dropping lines was more important than the results, but when it came to the one with whom I wanted to have the most intimate relationship, I was all but mute. I resorted to sending her notes with some wonderfully passionate lines, which apparently had little effect.

Realizing my inability to effectively communicate, I enjoyed Juanita primarily in my mind. I sat in study hall, daydreaming about how I would save the $1.25 it would cost to take Juanita on the boat ride through the amusement park's tunnel of love. I would get myself together, walk right up to her, show her the two tickets, and she would go with me on the ride. We would sit real close, and maybe I would get a chance to put my arm around her waist. After the ride, we would get a chance to walk alone through the park. I wouldn't have any trouble talking with her about the beatings we each had received as children, and Juanita just might give me a chance to take a close look at her one leg, right below the knee where there remained a scar from the time she fell on the pavement. I even daydreamed about us having children and how well we would treat them.

It took this mental face-to-face meeting with Juanita for me to understand and accept the fact that "Becoming Part of Her" triggered thoughts about "a very big one that got away." It would not be the last personal insight that I would glean from sifting through Omari's poetry.

The summers after tenth and eleventh grade, my uncles shared with me their favorite spots on the big river, starting up in Mount Union and including all of the spots between there and Lewistown, about thirty miles away. We fished spots with names invented and recognized by dedicated fishermen over the years, and in doing so, we hit just about every accessible part of the water.

Reflecting back on these times, I recognize how the challenges and countless exciting moments expanded all of our relationships beyond the merely familial. Besides the fishing experiences themselves, these were well-nurtured relationships, the kinds that could serve as infrastructure for the arks on which African American men could have safe passage when navigating through life. Unlike my relationship with Mr. Rhinehart, born of necessity and fostered by dependency, in my relationships with my uncles, we were woven together by the strands of common, positive experiences, the repeating of legendary stories that grew out of those experiences, and the participation in our late-night sitting-around-the-camp ritualistic behaviors. From these shared experiences came a sense of belonging that fed all of our souls.

6

THE WAY WE WERE RAISED

IT WAS the fall of Omari's senior year in high school, and while the two of us were watching a football game, his physical size reminded me that he would be leaving for college in a year. Not too long thereafter he would be a Daniel man. During a commercial, my mind turned to how my older brothers and I grew up believing that Daniel men were the ex emplars of men in stable African American families. Unlike many other African American and white men we knew while we were growing up in the projects, Daddy and his brother Youngie always worked, paid their bills, attended church, never got drunk, didn't gamble, and never chased women. Both emphasized the importance of higher education, ten of their eleven children earned at least one college degree, and all eleven became successful professional people. Feeling proud, and with the intent of inspiring him, I decided to share some Daniel men history with Omari.

"You know, my father was always with us but some of my friends weren't lucky enough to have their fathers living with them. Back then, much like today, I saw many examples of what Mama described as 'a poor gal who got messed up by a good for nothing man, and was left to raise a baby on her own.'"

Sounding unimpressed, and almost complaining, he responded,

"It's worse now. Most of the guys I know don't have fathers. Two of my friends have never received a Christmas present from their fathers, and most don't even know their fathers."

"That's true, but Daniel men were not only in the home. All around Johnstown, older people commented on how well Daddy helped Mama take care of our family. I can still hear our neighbor, Ms. Holmes, say, "Deacon Daniel sure helped Sis Grace raise those kids." She said it all the time, and so did others. All Daniel men cooked, and they were 'liberated men' long before the term became fashionable."

Still not seeming to appreciate the wonders of Daniel men, Omari looked at me and said,

"Mr. Matthews cooks, Marc's daddy cooks, Uncle Bob cooks, Granddad in California cooks, so what is so much about Daniel men cooking?"

A bit bothered, I raised my voice and went on a mild tirade.

"Daniel men didn't just cook! Everybody in Johnstown came to Daddy for advice. Even white people came to Daddy for advice about everything from family problems to church conflicts to problems with the police. White politicians came to talk with him when they were concerned with the 'Negro vote.' Once, with his personal testimony, Daddy prevented one of our family members from going to jail for involuntary manslaughter. On the day he spoke to the judge in court, people said Daddy wore his Masonic pins and gave the judge some sort of special handshake after he dismissed the case. If you wanted to get a job on the Conemaugh and Black Lick Railroad, Daddy could talk with the white 'higher ups' and get you a job as soon as there was an opening. In Virginia, everyone came to his brother Uncle Youngie for advice. Uncle Youngie . . ."

"If Daniel men are so great, then why do they have so much trouble raising their sons?"

"What do you mean?"

"Well, you're always fussing at me about things, and no matter what I do, you still find faults. So obviously you're not doing something right with me. And your father must have gotten something wrong with you."

"Now if you keep on talking about my father, I'm going to hurt you."

"Well, think about it. Your father always beat you or 'skinned' you, as you called it. And what about all of that going to church stuff? Since your father made you go to church so much, why didn't you stay out of trouble?"

Not having an answer, I ordered him to forget it and just watch the game. Mocking me, he answered, "No, I'm going to take a nap, and while I'm asleep, you think about answering me. In fact, I want you to write me an essay about Daniel men, and be sure to proofread it before you give it to me."

I ignored his taunt until a few years later when I read one of his poems, and ironically, "Daniel Men" returned me to this memory and his writing assignment.

Daniel Men

I had to see him at his worst
his belt slicing through the air
cutting into my bare legs
without remorse.
Like gravestone rubbings,
his veins emerged
small demonic hills
in his sweaty forehead.
As if possessed, he vented
his private hell on me.

I knew that he would have
preferred to drop dead while beating me
than watch me go on being wrong.

In his life he has seen many wrongs.
He saw men drinking with demons.
He saw men starving their
sweet brown babies.
He saw men disrespecting their
beautiful black wives
and it hurt his soul.
Now he saw his son doing wrong
and it dismembered his very essence.

My father beat me
and I hated him for it,
that is until my patches
of swollen skin had gone down.
Then I loved him for it,
because I understood why.
He beat me because
I had done wrong
and more importantly
he beat me because he loved me.
He loved me so much
that he would rather
kill me himself than
allow me to grow up wrong.

To understand this took time
but once I saw the light
I knew that his love for me
was beyond the natural realm.
I knew that I must be willing to beat my son,
be willing to let him see my worst,
let him feel my private hell, until he is able to hate me.
I must be willing to see one, or both
of us dead, before I allow him to dwell in darkness.
I must do all of this so that

when my son looks into the sky for help
he will see the faces of our ancestors
smiling down on him too,
and then he too will understand that to be worthy
of walking with the old Daniel Men in heaven
He will have to beat his son
harder than anyone before him
to make his son a good Daniel man
and have his love deemed supernatural.

Omari's retelling of his beatings and rationalization for my behavior as a "holy right" sickened me. I worried about my contribution to the perverse notion of fathers perpetually beating their sons. Although the sons turned out to be "good Daniel men," it pained me to hear my son adopt this version of "the ends justify the means." Omari's expression of this view was the worst beating I had ever received. Feeling distressed, I began to think about the way I and other African American children were raised during times when chores and corporal punishment were normative.

A typical Johnstown weekend began early Saturday morning with house-cleaning duties. Saturday evenings, Daddy made us polish our shoes and then line them up on the top of the steps for him to inspect. The toes of our shoes had to reflect like mirrors, and once Daddy deemed the shines satisfactory, he made us complete the job by putting liquid polish around the soles and heels. After our shoes passed inspection and were put under our bed, we placed on our dresser the socks, underwear, shirts, and neckties we were going to wear in the morning. Then came our Sunday school lessons.

I never studied public school books as much as I studied Sunday school books on Saturday evenings. An hour of studying our Sunday school lessons was followed by an oral quiz from Daddy. Too many missed questions by any one of us resulted in more study for all of us, and missed questions on the second oral quiz meant Daddy would send all of us to bed earlier than usual. When we passed his quizzes, Daddy sometimes gave us extra assignments. Once, he had us search several evenings, hours at a time, for the shortest verse in the Bible. Eventually, we found "Jesus wept." Under the best circumstances, my two older brothers and I had completed the drills and were in bed by eight o'clock on Saturday nights. By six o'clock Sunday morning, he had us out of bed, brushing our teeth, combing our heads, and dressing for church. He didn't believe in children or adults "laying up in the bed all hours of the morning." According to him, it led to laziness, and "laziness would kill you."

As soon as we got home from church, we ate our largest meal of the week. It was the one time for certain that the entire family sat at the table and meat was served. After Mama put the food on the table, and we sat in our usual places, Daddy's long prayers seemed like a continuation of church. He thanked God for more than I could ever remember, including things for which he had already thanked him during his prayers in church. He concluded with all of us saying "Amen," and finally we got to eat our usual Sunday dinner of Daddy's hamhock-seasoned kale or collard greens, and Mama's hot Parker House rolls made from scratch, fried chicken, potato salad, and either sweet potato pie or pineapple cake. After eating our dessert, we divided the work of cleaning up. We children took turns putting the food away, and washing, drying, and putting away the dishes. There was no such thing as clearing the table at a later time or drip-drying dishes, all of which Daddy and Mama considered to be laziness.

On Sunday afternoons, because Daddy believed more church was good for you and one of the evangelists worked on the railroad with him, we were sent to the recreational center where white evangelists came every Sunday to save the souls of poor colored children who lived in the projects. We were dismissed somewhere around five-thirty in the evening. By then, we had convinced the evangelists one more time that we would obey our parents, and when we grew up we would not drink, smoke, or fornicate because we had received Jesus Christ in our hearts. I was never able to understand exactly how people could have Jesus in their small hearts, given how big and powerful Jesus Christ was supposed to be in the scheme of things. I also couldn't understand why the evangelists kept calling him Jesus Christ, while all of the people at Mount Sinai Baptist Church just called him Jesus. And why did God send those white evangelists to meet with us week after week, given how easily we could trick them into believing we were the best little colored Christians on earth? During their prayers, we bowed our heads and said a "Yes Lord" here and there that helped convince them that they were saving our poor and downtrodden little souls. We could never have tricked Mama's evangelist friend, Sister Evelyn Moore, in that fashion. She would take one look at us, turn her dark face into a scowl, and start talking about how much the devil had a hold on us.

After the recreational center, the whole Sunday/God thing was just about over. When we got home, following a brief quiz on what we learned, Daddy wanted to know if we were ready for school. Being ready for school meant that homework had been completed and clean clothes had been laid out for Monday morning. School proved to be a much welcomed reprieve from the Saturday and Sunday regimen related to church. Our public school teachers never made us study anything as much as Daddy made us study the Bible, nor were they as demanding in general.

One dry, cold, winter Sunday morning after Daddy had gotten us up at the crack of dawn, made sure we were dressed properly, and fed us, we walked the mile and a half to downtown Johnstown. We waited for about fifteen minutes, then caught the streetcar to Franklin. We got off in Franklin, right in front of Papadakas's grocery store, and walked another mile and a half to the Mount Sinai Baptist Church. As we were walking along and complaining about being tired and cold, Daddy informed us that the walking was good for us and that the cold weather would make us tough. I thought he was just offering more excuses for the fact that just about everybody in Johnstown had some kind of used car except us. Mr. Jones worked the same job as Daddy, and he had a new car. Mr. Brown was on welfare, and he had a used car. Yet, Daddy claimed walking in the winter weather was good for us.

The only good I could see coming from being up so early and trudging along that bone-chilling cold morning was the fact that most of the kids my age were not up to see how ridiculous we looked. Most of them didn't go to church at all, and they could stay in bed as long as they wanted on Sunday mornings because their parents didn't get home from the Coke Plant Club or Club Twelve until a few hours before Daddy was getting us up to go to church. However, nothing of what was on my mind mattered to Daddy. As far as he was concerned, it was right for us to be walking. We quit complaining when Daddy told us that if we didn't walk a little faster, then we would be going to bed earlier that evening in order to get our "proper rest."

As we walked across the Franklin bridge heading to the church, we looked like three little ducklings being led by Daddy. I passed the time by trying to step in the occasional footsteps Sterlin left in the traces of powdery snow on the ground. I thought about the fact that Sunday school was supposed to be so good for us, but for reasons not known to me, Mama never attended Sunday school. She attended only the church part of the Sunday services. As the four of us pressed on without talking, I periodically would purposely bump into Sterlin who in turn bumped into Russell Jr. Then the whole routine would begin again like a chain reaction. Once, Sterlin bumped Russell Jr. too hard, and he gave Sterlin an elbow in the chest. When Sterlin elbowed me in the head, I slipped, and Daddy briefly looked back at the three of us. The brevity of his look caused ambiguity regarding whether he had seen any of the thrown elbows and was sending us a warning signal, or he had just happened to look back at that time. In any event, the immediate response was that all of the ducks got back in a row, and kept plodding along to church.

By the time we got to the church, my toes and fingers were almost numb. After we entered the church and I felt the coal-burning furnace's toasty warm air coming up through the floor vent, being in Sunday school felt really good. When Lou Helen came in with Deacon Davis, and she sat right in front of me, things got even better. The sweet aroma of her Dixie Peach hair grease and the beautiful contrast between her Hershey chocolate neck and the bright yellow lace that formed the collar on her blouse had my heart thumping as if I had just finished running a fifty-yard dash. This pleasant atmosphere changed, however, when the Superintendent of the Sunday school began to conduct a review of the morning's lesson.

As he reviewed the lesson, he went on and on about God having commanded us to " Honour thy father and mother. . . . That it may be well with thee, and thou mayest live long on the earth." Very few of the children were paying attention, and we all laughed at the hollow sound that occurred when Joe Jackson hit Shawn Matthews in the back of the head with the edge of a fan. With his eyes glowing as if some sort of spirit had hit him in the center of his forehead, Superintendent Moore told us sternly, "You children need to quit cutting up and listen to me and God's word, or you will find yourselves brought low in life. With God's blessing, your parents keep food on your table, and they keep shoes on your feet. You honor them no matter what, and God will bless you." My thoughts began drifting away from what he was saying as I considered how ridiculous it was for God to have said something as obvious as honor thy mother and father, when one whipping from either of them taught you to listen to them. And one of Daddy's lessons, as he put it, would "teach you a lesson for the rest of your life."

The Railroad

I stood silent,
staring,
vision blurred
by the mesh fence.
My small feet
were tired,
and the cold of the fence
crept through my gloves.

I arrived early,
daily,
trying to shame
the railroad into spitting
out my father
just a little before
it was officially time.

A figure appeared,
like Jonah,
from the railroad's mouth.
The figure,
now my father,
paused
a silent moment, waiting
for the gate to open.

His face was tired,
yet blank,
body hunched and abandoned
as he took my hand
with the calloused hand
he used instead of gloves
to keep the cold out.

We headed for home,
I could still smell on him
the pork chop sandwich that
my mother packed for lunch.
The stagnant air had
kept the smell from escaping.

The railroad watched us leave
with a smirk,
as if it knew
it was killing my father.

No matter what shift he worked on the railroad, Daddy always came home, in Mama's words, "broke down and tired." Mama was working just as hard in our home. Cooking, cleaning, canning, washing, ironing, child rearing, and periodically doing "day work" as a domestic in the home of a white family in the suburb of Westmount. One of her biggest burdens, however, stemmed from the fact that "Russell's children" were constantly "worrying her to death" by committing some form of bad conduct "no matter how well I try to raise them."

Having worked all day, Daddy really did not want to hear about our bad conduct or Mama's stroke symptoms, which she reported several times a week, when he got home from work. When he ended one of Mama's reports with, "I'll take care of them, Grace," we knew that we would experience an aspect of Hell on earth

No one in his right mind wanted to be "taken care of" by Daddy. Many times, as his belt swung through the air and landed on my body, I wondered if the whipping served to shut Mama out as much as to "teach me a lesson." When I thought about these incidents as an adult with children of my own, it seemed to me that part of the reason why I got "taught" so many lessons related to his working hard all day for low wages, never getting a chance to move beyond being a "broke down and tired" laborer who was always figuring out new ways to make ends meet from one payday to the next, and having a nagging wife who never let him forget these things. No matter why he decided to become such a great "teacher" for his children, and even though we quite often failed the "obey" part of the commandment, when the whippings occurred, I couldn't see anything right about Daddy whipping me.

One week, Daddy was working the three to eleven shift, the shift which usually left him in the worst form of " broke down and tired" because he always worked at home before he went to work. This particular day, before he had gone to work on the railroad, Daddy had worked on the roof of our house. He was pouring with sweat when he came down off the roof to eat lunch, take a nap, and leave for his three o'clock shift on the railroad. Before leaving for work, he and Mama had gotten into a discussion regarding bills. Daddy said he didn't want any more bills made by Mama, and Mama declared that she never made a bill that wasn't necessary. Mama said she just wanted all of the bills paid so that she didn't look like the rest of the welfare people who didn't pay their bills. Daddy ended the discussion by stating that he would handle all of his bills, and he left the table without completing his lunch. As tired and hungry as he was from working on the roof, not finishing his lunch was a truly bad sign. I was happy to be headed for a baseball game.

On the way to the game, Russell Jr. gave me a cap gun that he claimed to have found in some bushes. At the stadium, I hid it in the bleachers, and I never thought about it again until I walked in the house, and Mama yelled, "Where's that gun you stole from that child? You just won't listen to me, will you?" I knew there was no use explaining to her, and I knew that there would be no use explaining to Daddy. So I just said, "Mama, what gun? I don't know anything about a gun." Seeming to be no longer concerned with any response I might make, but confident the truth would be obtained, she casually said, "Well, we'll see what you know when Russell gets home. Since you are lying, go on to your room."

Sitting on the bed upstairs, I felt like a prisoner during his last hours on death row, with no hope for a last minute pardon. I knew that all Daddy would want when he got home that night was a big meal, peace, quiet, and sleep. The moment he came through the door, all that Mama would want would be to tell Daddy about how my not listening to her had led to stealing and lying. Russell Jr. and Sterlin eventually came to bed and fell asleep, but I was wide awake when Daddy got home around eleven-thirty. Had I known where to go, I would have run away. But there I lay, and my stomach quivered when I heard my prosecutor and judge utter, "Russell, wait until I tell you what Jack Lee did today."

Fear caused me to blank out much of what Mama said next. While I was breathing heavily and beginning to tremble, I heard Daddy end her summary of the case against me with, "Calm down Grace. I'll talk to that boy in a minute." I offered the silent but urgent prayer, "God, please let Daddy just talk to me!"

The next thing I heard was a slow and deliberate "boom, boom, boom, boom" as Daddy's heavy brogan-wearing feet made their way up the steps. With each step, I also heard the sounds of a hard working, tired and hungry, more than 250-pound, angry and frustrated black railroad man coming up the steps to teach me a few special lessons. Suddenly, the covers were snatched off the bed. There was a flurry of motion as Sterlin jumped out of the bed and moved into a corner over by the dresser. Russell Jr. jumped up and stood in the top corner of the bed against the wall. My instincts told me to run, but my better senses told me to remain lying in the bed. The smell of a railroad man's sweat intermingled with the funky odor in the spot on the bed where I hovered, practically paralyzed by fear. Before I could speak, Daddy started his "interview."

"So you ain't gonna listen to me and Grace, are you?"

"But, Daddy, but Daddy, I swear I'm going to listen."

"No, you're not. You can't even remember what you did today. This will teach you to steal and lie."

The blows came whizzing through the air so fast and hard that I didn't feel their impact, and not feeling their impact caused additional fear to roam freely throughout my body. The man I knew as my father disappeared, and momentarily, "I looked, and behold a pale horse: and his name that sat on him was Death, and Hell followed with him."

Daddy never, never, never liked to repeat himself, particularly when he asked a child to do something; preparing myself for the unknown terror that was sure to follow, my vision disappeared when he asked, "How many times am I going to have to talk to you?" Before I could answer, and as if he didn't want an answer from me, he repeated the question slowly, rhythmically. "How-many-times-am-I-going-to-have-to-talk-to-you?"

With my eyes shut and accepting my fate, I curled up like a porcupine in anticipation of the next several blows. As the maddening event continued to unfold, he seemed to be in a craze, talking to himself.

"I've talked to you and talked to you, but talking won't do you any good. I've never seen a child who needed to be told the same thing over, and over, and over. Well, when I get through skinning you this time, maybe that'll teach you a lesson. Boy, why don't you want to listen to me? Why do I have to always teach you a lesson?"

"Daddy, please! I don't need any more lessons! See, I'm listening now! I'm listening to every word you are saying! Daddy, I'm listening, I'm going to always listen to you!"

I brought forth a torrent of "have pity on me tears" as I tried to make my case for my new willingness to listen but before I could explain fully, his talking was over. Thunder and lightning hovered over me as I rolled, screamed, promised, begged, and tried to put the sheet between me and that snarling belt. If only it had been winter and I had been wearing long johns, they would have protected me more than my T-shirt and jockey shorts. After giving me more repetitions than I needed for his lesson to permeate my body, relief finally came. For some reason, Daddy decided to teach Russell Jr. a few lessons. Turning to him, he inquired, "Russell Jr., didn't I tell you to clean the bathroom today?"

"Yes sir."

"Then why was it a mess when I got here tonight?"

Standing at the top of the bed where he had witnessed my skinning, Russell Jr. started screaming about his innocent mistake.

"Daddy, I didn't remember."

"Well, this is going to teach you to remember."

Suddenly, the angry Python was wrapping around Russell Jr.'s legs, back and arms. His screaming, as if he was truly dying, helped deaden my pain a bit. Then, from the bottom of the steps, Mama yelled, "Stop Russell, please stop Russell, you're killing my children!" And in his usual, taking control fashion, he answered, "Grace, you let me handle this."

For once, I was glad when Mama didn't shut up and that we were "her children," not "Russell's children." Like a true guardian angel, she warned, "Russell, if you don't stop whipping my children, I'm going to call the law! I'll put the law on you the same way Annie Mae Henderson did for her husband. There ain't no sense in you going on like this, and if you don't stop, I'm calling the law."

Mama prevailed. After Daddy left the room, Russell Jr. was still whimpering and Sterlin lay totally silent in the bed, similar to how he had stood silently in the corner throughout the whole whipping ordeal. Apparently, he was on good behavior, and Daddy saw no need to give him some "medicine" too. I passed my hands up and down my legs; the welts on my thighs had developed a life of their own, quite sensitive to touch, making it hard to stay in one position too long. My mind took me fishing down at the little branch in Virginia. Wading in the water cooled the welts on my legs. When I dipped my bucket at a school of minnows, the splashing water relaxed my whole body. I fell asleep looking at three minnows in my aquarium.

Until now, I naively thought "that's just the way it was back then," and that a parent's right or duty to physically discipline his children was not "child abuse." Upon reflecting, it appears that violence begets violence. Starting with the brutality inflicted by slave masters, African Americans beat each other until beating became a glorified "cultural" experience whereby fathers beat their sons, daughters, and sometimes their wives. In addition, when I think about how Daddy taught us those "lessons," I believe that he was temporarily driven mad by the demons in his life. It was a long time, indeed years, after my "patches of swollen skin had gone down," before "I loved him for it" and understood a bit. But what a way to learn about love! Was it even love that I felt or just a nice label for the abuse in order to continue the relationship with my father? It took a tremendous amount of adult understanding to get from the cowering child in bed to being forty years old and wanting to do anything for Daddy because of all he had done to and for me. I was just thankful that it didn't take Omari forty years to learn how to cope with me.

Someone once said, "Poverty is the greatest background to come from, provided one can escape;" to this day, I don't know if I ever escaped completely from the effects of my father's whippings, or if I did, with what consequences. The more I searched for the deep meanings in Omari's "Daniel Men" poem, and the more I thought about all we had done while fishing, the more I came to believe that there had to be more effective ways to teach lessons to children. I realized too, that Omari learned a lot of good lessons from me without being whipped, and I remembered learning some extremely important lessons from Daddy without his skinnings. For the sake of future Daniel men, I sensed a duty to help Omari see this, too. I sat him down and told Omari other stories about my father.

"Because Daddy always 'made a way out of no way,' I never thought of myself as 'poor.' He never let us go hungry, although that was the fate shared by many of my friends. Because of his focus on the highest performance with our Sunday school lessons, I never believed that white public school students were smarter than me. His Saturday drills taught me the value of advanced preparation. Without hitting me, Daddy taught me that what I did to prepare myself, not what poverty and racism did to me, would have as much as anything else to do with who I became.

"At church, there were always Easter and Christmas Sunday school programs in which children performed. I was always frightened to death of this; for three years in a row, I broke into tears of terror before finishing the recital. Even though I had the poem memorized completely, it never failed that after taking my bow, stating the title of the poem, and saying one or two lines, my face flooded with tears. I couldn't even finish the four-liner,

> I don't know why you are looking at me
> I didn't come to stay
> I just came to say
> It's Happy Easter Day

"When I started crying, my legs froze from the fright, and I was unable to walk off the stage. No matter what the rest of the adults said about how it was a shame "that boy can't recite any better than that," or how much the other kids teased me, Daddy always came to my rescue. Without saying a word, he walked up to the stage, picked me up, held me in his strong arms, took me back to the Deacons' bench, put his arms around me, and made me feel as though I were special. When I was in third grade and peed in my pants while shopping with Daddy, he didn't chastise me. When we got home, he washed my pants, hung them up, and said, 'See, they will be as good as new.' I didn't stop peeing periodically in the bed until somewhere in third grade, and again Daddy would wash the sheets without comment, and he always gave me the impression that I wouldn't have to be embarrassed by him telling Mama what I had done. Now, I wonder if fewer skinnings would have caused me to pee less in the bed, to put less trust in the value of whipping." Omari sat silently, his head bowed, as I continued.

"Truthfully, I don't know what Daddy wanted me to learn from his skinnings. I did learn to fear him, to never get caught doing something against his will, and to literally jump when he said jump. I also found a way to lie to myself about loving him when I hated what he was doing to me. I should have never instilled in you this same disquieting disposition toward me. The only 'supernatural' things about this terrible legacy are that you were able to so quickly reverse this reality and to move from having such disturbing feelings about me. I'm just glad that I didn't skin you that day you locked the keys in the car and we lost a whole day of fishing, or the day you let all of our worms die in the hot sun instead of putting them in the cooler as I told you. After all that has happened to us, I hope that you will never cause your son to suffer the same emotional wreckage by skinning him when talking, holding, and supporting is what he and so many other African American men need."

Noting that he was sitting in silence, I wondered if Omari had stopped listening to me long ago—not just now, but years ago. I was so troubled by what I had just said that I joined the silence. Years later, much like the Father's Day letter, I received the following poem and note from Omari after his wife gave birth to their son, Javon Tyson Daniel.

After the Birth of a Daniel Man

My victim screams for me at two A.M.
I stuff rubber in his mouth to muffle his cries,
then I stalk my pillow.

My victim screams for me at four A.M.
I stuff a nipple in his mouth for silence,
so I can stalk my pillow.

My victim screams for me at five A.M.
I stuff stories in his ears because
my pillow and dreams have eluded me.

I tell Javon about his great grandfather
who beat his grandfather who
beat his father who now
wonders if he will beat him
to fulfill the Daniel Man prophecy
he once held so dear.

Cradling Javon's sacred flesh,
I ask him if I will be able

to defile his temple?
He has no answers—
Javon knows no words—
He only knows to grin
and cling to his father,
like his father clung
to his grandfather's rope,
like his grandfather clung
to his great grandfather's Sunday suit—
like his father clings to him now,
It is the clench the Lord gave Jesus
before sacrificing him to the world.

I want the strength to be better than God.
I want the power to save Javon from the belt
save him from his destiny as a "Daniel man"
save him from having to wait like Jesus for his father
to betray his body for the greater good.

DADDY,

I heard you that day we sat in silence Please continue to help me to be stronger than "Daniel men" ever dreamed. I gave Javon a tiny fishing rod. When will you be ready to go?

OMARI

7

THE TIES THAT BIND

First Steps

Soon I was able to walk behind my father,
the rope would prod me along by
cutting into my sides
when it felt me falling too far behind.
I always hated the first step into the river.
When the water crept over my boots,
my buttocks clenched and shook violently.
I fell many times, the waters would wash over my soul
until my father pulled me up.

When I was eight, the cord was cut.
I was navigating the banks of the Juniata by myself
My father's long strides would carry him away.
Finally, he would yell, and I would struggle to catch up.
I dreamed of being able to keep up.
A few years later, I could keep up for the first few hours,

but the pelting sun and the weight of my boots
made me drift further and further back.

At twenty, I am able to go stride for stride.
I am no longer a burden, but more of a friend, a competitor.
Every time I go back to those primordial waters,
I look at my reflection and realize
how far I have come.

IT WAS really satisfying to see how independent Omari had become as a young man, how in some ways he was taking the lead as opposed to following me. One day, while wading in the middle of the river, I stopped to fish one of my favorite bass holes. Omari knew how much I liked the spot; it was one of those places on the river where I stood silently, enjoying the peacefulness of the water flowing by my waist, the hundreds of minnows darting around my legs, the two or three evergreens growing out the side of a reddish brown rocky hillside, the natural isolation of the area, and the occasional strike of a big fish. Though the first cast was usually his, Omari watched as I cast my line out, then continued wading toward a spot a few yards to my left. After about a half hour, I turned to tell him that it was time to move, but saw that he had waded about thirty yards away, where he was fighting a fish in a place we usually bypassed. The fish made a jump, and Omari began to take up the slack in his line as soon as the fish reentered the water. Slowly, he brought the fish in, took it off the hook, then gently released it like a veteran catch and release fisherman. Knowing that he had found the action, I waded to where he was standing in water deep enough to touch his elbows, and asked, "Why did you release that fish? My spot only got me a couple of baby bass. You're over here in water over your waist, letting nice ones go that we need for lunch today. What's going on?" He retrieved his bait, and moved a few steps so that I could get positioned for casting. Then, without looking at me, and in a somewhat instructional tone, he said, "This water is pretty deep. That fish hit before I could work my bait to the deepest water. I'm sure I can catch one or two nicer fish if I wade a little further. Like Uncle William always says, there's more where that one came from."

Instinctively, I was tempted to tell Omari to be careful as he inched into deeper water. Instead, I made a precise cast to a spot about ten yards in front of him. He simply smiled, seeming to know that I was quietly suggesting that he not wade into deeper water as opposed to poaching the area in front of him. Taking my hint, he took several steps to the side, and made a cast longer than mine. An even larger smile appeared on his face when another of his casts was followed by the strike of a huge fish, just after I had made several more casts without getting a bite. Omari, too, had a lesson or two he wanted to teach, points he wanted to prove.

Later in the day, we met up with Henry Harris. As the three of us headed across some swift water, instead of the young child struggling to keep up with the older men, Omari's strong, athletic legs were easily out-distancing us. Looking back at me, he asked, "You need some help cross-ing through here? Be careful, this water's running real fast. You can hold on to my belt if you want." Not wanting to give credence to his last com-ment, I answered, "You go ahead. I'm fishing with Henry. We'll circle below and meet you down the river where that big sycamore tree hangs over the water."

Omari and I first began fishing the Juniata River the summer he com-pleted kindergarten. Though he would never admit to being afraid, it was clear that he preferred not putting slimy wiggling night crawlers on his hooks. I wasn't sure of whether he was afraid of the worms, being stuck by the hooks, or both, but to save time and to avoid dealing with his emotional issues, I baited his hooks for him. Once while we were sitting on the bank, Omari dumped a worm on the ground, and attempted to stick it without his fingers touching it. The worm was especially lively, and after several minutes of watching this frustrating comedy, I put the thing on his hook, cast out into the current, and handed the rod to him.

During the early years, before we entered the river, I joined Omari to me with an eight-foot piece of rope that trainers use to lead race-horses. I tied an end of the rope securely around each of our waists, and it functioned as a safety line for him. Years earlier, my younger brother Stephen had been on the other end of that rope, and after Omari, my sister's son Daniel, and Stephen's son Bryan would take their places on the other end.

On first fishing trips, novices always proclaimed they didn't need to be tied to the rope, but after being in water up to their waists and having slipped a few times, the newcomers usually clung to it as a true lifeline. The first time I put the rope on Omari, he protested, "I don't need that rope tied to me. Last week, the lifeguard let me dive into the deep end of the pool and swim out."

"Yeah, but this river ain't no swimming pool, and I'm the lifeguard here."

"But you should have seen me. I dove into the deep about five times in a row. Nothing happened. So why do I need this rope on me?"

Before I could answer, he slipped, water came over his shoulders, the current spun him around, and I quickly used the rope to pull him to his feet. The rest of the day, as we waded, Omari held the rope tightly with both hands. When we stopped to fish, he was reluctant to let go and take his fishing rod.

Initially, when we got to the edge of the river and the rope was secured around our waists, I often had Omari climb up on my shoulders, to save time getting from one fishing spot to the next, and spare Omari the early morning wake-up calls from the cold water. With my child sitting on my shoulders, I carefully waded down the river's edge, holding our two fishing rods, and stopped several yards before a drop off. Then I put him on the bank, I remained in the water, and we began to fish, allowing our bait to float downstream into the deeper water. Initially, fear of falling caused Omari's legs to lock around my shoulders, but by the third or fourth trip, he fortunately was no longer afraid, and I no longer felt like two miniature pythons were struggling on my back.

As I waded to large rocks on which Omari could safely sit or stand, I instructed, "Look at that dark green water off to my left. The water is darker because it is deeper."

"How deep?"

"I don't know for sure, but it's over your head. If you cast slightly up-stream and allow the bait to drift back downstream into that deeper water, you'll probably get one because the fish are sitting in there feeding. Let's stop and try it."

Using his rod, I made a cast above the deep water, and handed it to Omari. After he got a few nibbles and missed the fish by jerking his line too soon, I used my fingers to show him how fish often approach by quickly grabbing the bait and letting it go before they take the bait com-pletely into their mouths. Then I cautioned, "So take your time. Let the fish run with it a bit, and when you see your line moving through the water, then set your hook by jerking up on your rod in the opposite di-rection from which the fish is swimming."

Although he usually listened or at least gave the appearance of lis-tening, I'm sure he often hoped that I would shut up and just let him fish. Once something that I told him worked, however, he would repeat it over and over. I will never forget the twinkle in his eye the day we were sitting on the bank and I glanced over just in time to see him watching his line move through the water. He got up on one knee, expertly set the hook, and as I noticed his triumphant smile, I felt my own. When he could cast accurately for a good distance, I showed him how to cast far out into fast water, and to retrieve slowly until his bait reached the slower water. The first time that he tried this, a big channel catfish with a sag-ging belly pounced on his crab; to this day, he loves this maneuver, call-ing it the "Omari Retrieve."

Each year, each trip, each new stretch of the river, I let Omari wade a little more. When he slipped on the smooth sandstones of the riverbed and fell into water up to his neck, I quickly pulled him back up before the water could get in his face. It was very important that he not get frightened at an early age and get turned off to this form of fishing. As we crossed a swift current, in addition to the rope's support, I had him hold onto an extra belt I wore around my waist for his support, and I always kept him upstream so that I could scoop him up if he fell and the water began to carry him down stream. By the end of his grade-school years, I permitted him to extend the rope as far as it would stretch from me. I knew each spot I waded with him so well that I could navigate with the feel of my feet. This was especially helpful when the water was muddy, and I could test depths only by using my feet to feel for familiar landmarks.

For five or six years, it seemed as though I spent more time teaching him about the nature of the river, safety in the water and the woods, and the feeding habits of the fish than I actually spent fishing. Often, just as I was getting ready to do some serious fishing of my own, Omari needed help with things such as tying on a hook, baiting his hook, getting his hook off a snag, taking a fish off the hook, or unraveling his line which had formed a miniature bird's nest after one of his faulty casts. And my ultimate frustration came during those times when we had made our way through thick woods, gone a good distance across the river, and before we could fish, he pitifully informed me, "Daddy, I need to go sit on the toilet."

One day the fishing was poor, and Omari kept complaining about the heat and the May flies, though he had already sprayed enough insect repellant on himself that he glistened. I was regretting the fact that he was with me when, with the voice of a child's curiosity about something truly mysterious, he said very slowly and softly, "Daddy, something is pulling my line." Annoyed with both the flies and him, I said half angrily, "Don't tell me about something pulling your line. Set your hook! Set it now before the fish gets away!"

Standing there flabbergasted, he never did set his hook, and in the meantime, the hungry fish swallowed his bait and made a dash across the river. Now, he had the problem of bringing a large fish back across the current. However, as his rod remained bent downward, Omari confidently looked up at me and said, "I got him!" and added, "Looks like he is bigger than anything you caught today."

I put the fish on his stringer, and began casting to a likely place for fish to be holding. A few minutes later, Omari had another fish on the line, and he worked it for at least five minutes. I concentrated on working my bait through the water, pretending to be totally unconcerned with what he was doing. Finally, the fish was at his knees; it was clear that he would not be able to land the still-active fish while maintaining his balance in the water and fanning flies. I relented a bit.

"Lean against me while I take the fish off your hook. Keep your rod pointed up in the air, or the fish will get away. After I get this fish off, I'm going to put a crab on your hook because I think some big bass are in here."

Now oblivious to the May flies, Omari shouted, "Hurry up! I want to get another one!"

"You're going to have to get another one."

Before he could ask why, I gave him a short glimpse of the huge rock bass, which I then dropped into the water. I wanted him to get over his fear of the flopping fish. As Omari stood speechless, I explained, "The sooner you learn to take the fish off your hook and put them on your stringer, the sooner you won't have to worry about me accidentally dropping one of your fish back into the river."

His sadness was short-lived, for as soon as I baited his hook, he made a long cast and waited intensely for another bite. In less than two minutes, he was complaining, "I thought that crab you put on was going to do so much." Irked by his comment, I explained, "If you'd just be patient and concentrate on what you are supposed to be doing, maybe you would catch a big one. Look, I've got a big one on now. He hit a crab, just like the one I gave you." While watching me, a big fish began to run with Omari's bait and he exclaimed, "I've got him!" His rod bent to the maximum and suddenly his line snapped. Returning to teaching him, I said, "You had him, huh? Hold your rod over here so that I can tie on another hook, and I'm going to give you one more of my good crabs."

About a dozen fish and thirty minutes later, I suggested it was time to move on to another spot. By now, his small body had adjusted to the water temperature. The flies all over his hat were no longer bothering him. Since I knew the water would become increasingly shallow as we approached the island we were headed for, I let him walk in order that he might gain additional wading experience. Preoccupied with what he had caught and what he might catch over on the island, he followed me on the rope, unconcerned with the fact that the water was considerably above his waist.

I was hard on Omari as I taught him to fish, but wading the river was very dangerous, and with one misstep, you could be in water over your head, weighted down by a stringer of fish, boots filled with water, and fishing tackle. I knew of two recent drownings, and the thought of something bad happening to my son was so overwhelming that I became compulsive with regard to making sure that he learned everything about wading safely, and still had fun. Part of my unwinding at the end of a fishing day consisted of being back at camp and reflecting on the fact that Omari was safe and sound.

One time the rope really did prove to be a lifeline. This particular day, after wading out into water over my waist, Omari got off my shoulders and sat on a huge rock. The water was just high enough to trickle over the rock, and so he had a seat as well as a form of natural air conditioning. A few feet in front of the rock, the water was swift and over six feet deep. After fishing for about fifteen minutes without a bite, we were wondering whether the long walk down to the spot had been worth the trouble. As I was scouting for the next place to fish, suddenly his rod bent over, and his line went sideways and upstream. As he fought the fish, its pull, the flowing water, and the slippery top of the rock combined to cause him to slide into the river. Except for the rope, the swift current would have swept him away in seconds.

His feet clearly were not touching the ground as he drifted into the current, and, dangling on the end of the rope, he reminded me of astronauts in space. Fortunately, he didn't tumble; his knee-high boots, full of water, helped to keep his feet down. The rope got tight. Neither of us spoke as I began to reel Omari in while he simultaneously pumped and reeled the bass like a pro, rather than a grade-school child. As he fought the fish, I gradually worked my way toward the riverbank, all the time using the rope to pull him closer to me. When he found himself in water shallow enough to plant his feet, he continued his fight with the fish, and I made a little slack in the rope to let him fight it on his own. This contest of fish, child, and rope affected me profoundly.

While Omari stood on the riverbank, admiring the huge bass wiggling slowly in the weeds at the river's edge, a tremendous sense of both terror and excitement overcame me. The flurry of events left me contemplating the possibility of losing Omari to the river, taking precedence over my reactions to him having caught the largest bass of his life (it was, indeed, one of the largest bass I had ever seen come out of this river). I flinched at my concern for the contest between the child and the fish over the safety of my son, and my mind was flooded with images; there were other times Omari had slipped and fallen into the water but I had not fully attended, I had simply pulled him up by the rope. Some of those times, the situations seemed funny and we had laughed them off, but now I wondered if any of them had really been funny at all.

My thoughts continued along this scary path; all of the times I had depended on the rope to rescue my son, I never thought about the possibility of the rope breaking or a knot failing. We both trusted the rope, and he trusted me so much that, when the trophy bass pulled him off the rock and into the deep, swift water, he continued to focus on the fish. I was overwhelmed by the extent to which Omari assumed that the rope and I were all of the security he needed, and the extent to which I had believed the same thing.

Omari's body slowly came into focus even though I had been staring at him all along. He was still standing there, admiring the fish, not realizing that no fish was worth risking his life. As much as I wanted him to learn from this incident, to talk about it, I was unable to speak, shaken by my own realizations and caught in the crosscurrents of fear, guilt, and excitement.

The rope incident continued to haunt me, and, throughout the rest of his childhood, I always kept an extra eye on Omari when we fished. Years later, I used my reading of "First Steps" as an opportunity to discuss with him the role of a metaphorical rope in the lives of the many African American children drowning in bad social circumstances. Returning from one fishing trip while he was a graduate student, I reflected back to the rope incident and pondered the terrible thing that could have happened. Then I reminded Omari of the situation, how the rope had saved him that day, and I asked him to tell me about the "ropes" in the lives of the inner-city African American children whom he taught during the summer. I was anxiously searching for ways to make meaning of our relationship for other African American males, and so I was really disturbed when he seemed to make light of my question by replying, "Tell you what? What is it that you don't understand? You're always making something big out of something obvious."

"You're the one who wrote about an umbilical cord. I never thought of the rope that way."

"Okay, now that you have, what do you make of it?"

I couldn't believe him. His analogy had sent me spiraling into deep thoughts about complex African American male relationships. Since I was feverishly searching for answers and desperately wanted to know how he would extend his metaphor, I controlled myself. Calmly, I replied, "I've thought about it, but before I write anything, I want to know what you'd say about the ropes in these kids' lives." What he then said caused me to have a rush of excitement, and I took as many mental notes as possible while he held forth.

"First of all, some don't have any ropes and that's why they die young. For a lot of them, their supposed ropes are their gangs. Their gangs are supposed to save them from the bad currents in their lives. The gangs give them brother-to-brother and substitute father relationships. If they're not in gangs, sometimes the rope for an eight- or nine-year-old is a relationship with a twelve- or thirteen-year-old brother or sister. But the trouble is that the person on the other end of that rope often doesn't know too much more than the young child does, or what the thirteen-year old does know is something to get him and his little brother into all kinds of trouble, and maybe killed. And the people on the other end of these kids' ropes don't know as much about the streets as you know about the river, although they think they know everything about the streets. That's why so many of them end up dead, and you'd never let anyone drown. Those kids you're worried about might get killed by the very person who is supposed to be protecting them. And no matter what, they don't get the proper nourishment from their umbilical cords."

With that, Omari slumped into his seat and, as if to signal "end of discussion," pulled his hat over his eyes. I sped along silently, engaging thoughts about ways to develop strong ropes for African American men. It occurred to me that "ropes" might be rituals designed to acknowledge the different stages of African American males' growth and development, and there had to be an extra special ritual when they got off "the rope" and became men.

Now, as I was lying in my bunk quite pleased with the independence he had achieved, it was clear to me that, over the years, a young father had helped nourish a child to adulthood, a middle-aged father was now being nourished by his child. Signs of the changes flowed through my mind as I recalled a day on which, when we waded over to the bank, Omari quickly and effortlessly climbed out of the river, and extended his hand to pull me up the riverbank. Then, too, responsibilities increasingly shifted to Omari as he began to do most of the driving once we got to the camp, and he determined where the best places were to fish on a given day. There is both self-respect and mutual respect for our acquired fishing skills.

Now, when we go fishing behind the school yard, I fish the riffles upstream, and Omari fishes the deep bass hole about fifty yards down. Despite the physical separation, I feel our connectedness and sense his moves and moods, as he casts, waits, sets the hook, looks slightly over his shoulder toward me to see if I have noticed, and reels in the fish. Like him, I tried to develop relationships with several other fishing buddies after Omari went away to college, but as is the case with him, fishing with others is "just fishing." Fishing together is affirmation. It came to me slowly, but finally I saw that the "together" was the most important part of fishing, and it was a pleasant and precious realization that, in the morning, we would get yet another chance to share the experience.

8

LET'S GO!

OMARI WAS in junior high school, and I hoped the coming Memorial Day weekend would be the first time this year we would have the full complement of our camp's members: Uncle Nash, Uncle William, my brother Stephen, my friend Henry Harris, and several other men who had been part of this group for years. Full of excitement, I telephoned Uncle William to find out if he and Uncle Nash were going to meet us at the camp for the weekend. He answered after one ring, and full of zest, asked,

"Where the hell you been boy? We've been waiting for you to call. All of the guys are looking forward to the weekend."

"Gee, it's just Tuesday evening. I'd have called earlier, but I didn't think you would know who all could make it by then."

"Make it? Nash and I've been planning since last week. You just be there with your son as soon as you can on Friday."

"That's all I wanted to hear. See you Friday."

I tended to forget that these outings were as exciting for everyone else as they were for me, and that a three-day fishing trip actually began with several days of advance planning. First, I had to design an escape plan from my administrative and faculty responsibilities at the university. If my work schedule didn't permit me to get away, then I found ways to make the work fit the weekend. Sometimes I got ill with a "swimming in my head," an illness I borrowed from my mother that proved to be full of mystery for and elicit concern from my colleagues. I also had more than a few out of town "emergencies" that began on Fridays. When my university colleagues became too suspicious of my weekend emergencies, I established a "field station" on the Juniata River where I conducted my "field research." Eventually, of course, the entire fishing game plan was exposed and it became a given that, having taken care of everything on my week's agenda by Thursday, I'd be out of there on Friday.

I liked to leave between three and four in the morning, when there was little traffic, so as to get to the river while the fish were feeding. The night before we left, I usually went to bed early, drifting close to deep sleep while thinking about important things: the river's probable water conditions—high or low; muddy, clear, brown, or brown-green; swift or meandering; and late May cool to cold as opposed to the soft welcoming warmer water temperatures of the usually hot and dry month of July. Depending on the river's conditions, I knew where it would be best to fish and what bait to use. Once when I tried to give Omari advance explanations regarding the river's various conditions, he showed his growing independence of thought and impatience with these lessons asking, "Why can't we just wait until we get there and find out about the river's condition? Don't you always have enough different bait for every condition?" He just didn't get the thrill of detailed planning and anxious anticipation yet. Maybe in time. I also wanted him to become an expert fisherman, and a good part of that had to do with knowing a lot about all of the relevant variables.

Regardless of what time I set my clock, I always awakened a half hour or so ahead of time; Omari said that I "woke the alarm," because I was caught up in fishing fever. I usually pushed the button before the alarm sounded as a matter of courtesy to Jerri, although it was never enough to prevent her from being awakened. This particular Friday morning, Jerri mumbled something suggestive of the fact that, once again, she had been awakened at what she viewed as a most "impossible hour." As I left the bedroom, her complaining mumbles were followed by, "Have a good time," and, before I could appreciate the warmth of the sentiment, an emphatic "Drive safely!"

There were historical realities but also subsequent fictions that circulated regarding "Jack's driving." My extended family knew that I had been the first to accumulate enough speeding tickets to be required to attend drivers' training school. How fast I had been driving, the amounts of the fines, and other details varied with the storyteller. This family mythology was enriched by the accident in which I fell asleep, smashed into a telephone pole, rolled over, totaled the car, broke both arms and received a number of head and facial lacerations. Reports on my driving on fishing trips added to the ever-growing legend. I could never wait to get to where I was going fishing; more than once as I was speeding along, I fantasized about having a helicopter that would drop me into my favorite spot in a matter of minutes, and this eagerness was transmitted to the car's gas pedal.

Once, when Omari was still a grade school student, we fished with my brother Stephen and his wife Renae for about an hour and a half in the rain before driving to a favorite bend in the river near McVeytown. As we swung into a J-shaped curve, my Oldsmobile skidded on the wet pavement, slammed into the guardrail, and bounced back into the road. When I slid out of the curve and stepped on the gas, Renae said nervously, "Did you see that Stephen? He didn't even stop. I don't believe it. Your brother didn't even stop after he wrecked his new car." Completely understanding me, Stephen simply answered, "Don't worry, he's just trying to get to the next spot." I said nothing in response, and sped to McVeytown where I knew more hungry fish were waiting. We fished in the rain for another hour or so. By then, the rain had soaked through my fishing vest, jacket, and shirt. We were still catching fish when we heard distant thunder, and with no sign of the rain ending, we decided to quit for the day.

After the drive from Mount Union to Johnstown, we unloaded the car, cleaned the fish and ourselves, and sat with Mama in the living room talking about the day, while Daddy cooked. Seemingly out of nowhere, Omari said, "Grandma, Daddy almost killed me today!" "Say what?" Mama responded, not as a question but a demand for Omari to tell more. Looking like a vulnerable little Bambi, Omari said in his most childlike voice, "Daddy almost killed me today when he wrecked. Grandma, I thought I was going to die." This produced a small demonstration of what we called "getting Mama started." While glaring at me, Mama said to Omari,

"Lawd, have mercy! Baby, tell Grandma what happened! Lawd, Russell. Listen! Tell me, son."

"Daddy was speeding, and he went into a curve so fast that he almost turned over and killed me. Aunt Renae tried to get him to slow down, but he wouldn't listen. He just kept on speeding, and I couldn't tell how fast he was going. I was scared to death. If the guardrail hadn't been there, he would have turned over and killed me."

"Jack Lee, Lawd son, why you want to try to kill my grandchild? I've told you he's too young to be up there at that camp. You don't need to be up there yourself with those other men and the dirt they are doing. You know what they say about that one old man going with that nasty young girl. You know you are married, and this child is so young. I'm going to tell Jerri to keep both of you out from up there! Russell! You hear me, Russell? Jack Lee almost killed this child. I'd call Jerri now, but I don't want to worry her to death. Russell, should I call?"

When Daddy didn't answer, Mama headed for the kitchen. Seeing the anger in my face, Omari ran behind her. Stephen and Renae broke into laughter as I faked jumping up to go after him. Reports like Omari's, combined with my mother's hysterical reactions, grew into tales of legendary proportions. By the time the story got back to Uncle William, he called to see if I had "totaled" my car.

This morning, after promising Jerri that I'd drive safely, I made my way in the dark to Omari's room, pulled back his covers, and he looked at me with a "you again" frown. Before he could complain, I gently ordered, "Omari, let's go. The fish aren't going to wait for us. I'm going to take my shower and then go downstairs to check on things." Without opening his eyes, he muttered, "Uuum hummm," and with that, he eased to the side of his bed. Then he sat there staring at me. Satisfied that he would continue to get ready, I headed to the shower for my final wake-up call. In addition to the fact that the cool shower prepared me to be alert for driving, I took great satisfaction in the fact that this would be my last shower until I returned in a few days. It was also ritualistic; a washing away of whatever I wanted to forget in Pittsburgh.

By the time that Omari showered, came downstairs, and dragged himself into the car, I noticed that we were running a little late, but decided to check the trunk for the last time. From the front of the car came a sarcastic, "Let's go. You said the fish wouldn't wait. Besides, you checked all of that stuff last night." Joining what seemed to be the beginning of the day's competition, I reached back for some old wisdom and said, "Yeah, but Mama always said, 'Look ahead and prepare, rather than look back in despair.' So, I'm making sure we have everything we need." Seeking to be dismissive, he answered, "I know, I know. And down on the Virginia plantation you and your brothers had things really hard, and all of us children now have a much easier time of everything."

Ignoring him, I continued my inspection, checking the backseat to make sure that everything was in order. With the engine running, I double-checked the gas level, and noting that it was full, I eased out of the driveway. Before I had gone three miles on the parkway, my speedometer was nudging seventy. I looked over at Omari, curled up like a puppy in the passenger seat. He had placed one of Mama's handmade pillows in his desired resting position, and put in one of his favorite tapes. Some time during junior high school, Omari's musical tastes had veered from popular soul music into rap, its messages too fast for me to pick up except for the very clear profanity and misogyny, which troubled me. As his music played, I drove through the dark, wondering.

The lyrics were enough to make me momentarily forget about fishing, as I wondered why so much rap talked about "killing muthafuckas" and "dissin' hoes and bitches." Then I became angry, recalling the day, Omari had had the nerve to play this vulgarity in the presence of his mother. I hadn't known how to react: to play the understanding parent, or tell him what I really thought about his music and his disrespect for Jerri. I had ejected the tape, and put on one of my favorite stations. I saw little redeeming value in rap music, and I wondered why he was so attracted to it. Was it because we had not exposed him enough to "good' literature and music, merely peer pressure, or was there a message I was totally missing? Omari played a rap for me once that was supposed to have a positive message. I tried to be convinced but sat in agony, listening to "Goddamn, I'm proud to be black y'all, and that's a fact y'all, and if you try to take what's mine, I'll take it back."

I couldn't get it. I never said "damn" in the presence of my parents; Daddy and Mama would have "set me on fire" with a belt. Now, sitting at a red light, just thirty minutes into my trip, I could hear someone on the tape screaming about "fucking this" and "fucking that," and I was reminded of the Last Poets, a group from my revolutionary days, who talked about "niggers fucking everything but fuck itself." Rather than add criticism of his music tastes to my ongoing discussions regarding his academic work, I sought refuge in thinking our musical differences might merely reflect the generation gap. After all, my parents were decent Christian folk, a Mason and an Eastern Star, and during the fifties were shocked when they heard me singing along as the local radio station played "Annie Had a Baby" and "Work with Me Henry."

These days, I never needed a cup of coffee as a stimulant for our early morning drives, and this morning was no different. The sounds of Omari's tapes were like toothpicks in my eyelids, keeping me wide-eyed as I sped through the early morning hours. After the light turned green and I picked up considerable speed, Omari turned up the volume, declaring that the particular song was one of his favorites. Since his whole generation seemed to be equally absorbed in "hip-hop" and "gangsta rap," I asked, "What is so deep about that song and rap in general? All that I hear is boom, boom, boom and a lot of cursing."

"Boom, boom, boom? What are you listening to with that old James Brown tape where he just keeps going please, please, please?"

"See. You're ignorant. James Brown also sang, 'I'm black and I'm proud,' and Aretha sang about 'respect', and Curtis Mayfield's 'Keep on Pushin'' became a theme song for the Movement. Their music had a lot of social relevance."

"But, see, that's what you're missing. You keep talking about people our age speaking up about race and everything. Well, rappers are speaking up, dealing with today's struggle. You say you want to understand us better, but if you don't understand rap, you're never going to understand us."

"Maybe so, but, why do they have to curse so much? Since when did music become cursing? Not one of them can sing like Ray Charles or Aretha."

"Well, say what you want. They've influenced a lot of people my age."

We didn't resolve anything that morning, but several years later, "As a Poet" convinced me that Omari had come to see some of what I was saying back then.

As a Poet

I wish I could say
that it was Miles Davis
some blues or
maybe some deep black
motown love
that has driven me
to write this poem
but I can't,

it was
bassridden rhythm
of a gangsta rappa;
and a sista,
Levita
was her name,
a sista,
who
is angry
angry at her sisters
who can't see that
these things
these beasts
these others
that their black men
are calling bitches
in their songs
in their dreams
in passing
and
in their play?
are really female
female and black
black and female
and beautiful
black, beautiful
and female
and angry
angrily beautiful
beautifully black
and angry
and female
and female
and
female

like
them
yet
still
as a poet
I wish I could say
that it was Miles Davis
or some blues
that has driven me
to write this poem.
but not dese blues
not your blues Levita
cause this poem is not mine
it's yours.

After our music discussion, Omari went to sleep. I turned off his tape and selected a talk show. In considerably less time than the normal three hours, we arrived in Mount Union and went to catch hellgrammites and crayfish in a little five-foot wide stream near our camp. If you weren't fully awake at this part of the morning, you soon would be, stepping into cold water at six-thirty and "kicking" the creatures into the four-by-five-foot net fastened on two poles. During his first years of fishing, Omari just watched as I and others worked in Crab Creek as we called it; by fourth or fifth grade, he stood downstream helping to hold the net, and by the time he was in junior high, Omari graduated to alternating with me and others in terms of who held the net and who dragged their feet and kicked the bait into the net. Initially, Omari hadn't liked the pinching part, but realizing hellgrammites' strong appeal to black bass, as well as a variety of big fish, he soon got with the program. Enjoying myself so much this particular morning, I decided to do all of the kicking, with toe bruises to show later that night. About a half hour later, with our bait cans brimming with hellgrammites and crabs, we got in the car and headed over to our camp.

Our fishing camp was nestled between intermittent patches of maple and oak trees, blackberry bushes, and clumps of cattails in the quiet, all white, country town called Kistler. The little town never seemed to come to life until the good old boys were flying up and down its narrow country roads at night. They'd roar past us as if they were practicing for the Indianapolis 500, drunk and hollering out their car windows as if they were in a rodeo. Although we temporary residents were the only people of color, there was little racial conflict. There had been a time when whites in Kistler wouldn't swim in the same area of the river that African Americans used. In any case, whites never bothered us, and over the years, they seemed to be glad to see us come and enjoy ourselves. Occasionally we shared with them our success in fishing, sometimes stopping to show the white fisherman our catch of the day.

As I pulled into camp, I saw three cars parked in an irregular pattern, and no one had gotten out of bed. Knowing that Uncle Nash sometimes kept a loaded rifle under his bunk, I cautiously approached the front bus door while Omari stayed in the car. The empty beer cans, the less than half-full bottle of Gordon's gin, the empty Canadian Club bottle, the partially eaten sandwiches, and the open loaf of bread and jar of mustard sitting on the outside table suggested that there had been some happy campers Thursday night. As I got to the top of the bus steps and opened the door, I heard several people snoring; first came a series of heavy, jerky snorts from the front of the bus, then a long, trembling inhale that was followed by a sharp hissing coming from somewhere in the back. Hearing all of this, I plugged in the front light, and a groggy voice inquired, "Who the hell turned on that Goddamn light this early in the morning?" I answered, "The Bassman is here! Let's go you guys! I thought we were going to do some serious fishing, and all you old men are laying up here in bed." A hung-over Uncle Nash drawled, "It ain't nobody but that damn Jack Lee. Who else is going to act the fool like that but somebody with too damn much education?"

I looked back, and saw Omari had entered the bus with a big smile on his face. Things were nearly perfect. In addition to Uncles Nash and William, Mr. Revere and Mr. Stevenson were in the bus. As a sign of respect toward these two longest-standing camp members, everyone younger than them used "Mr." when referring to these men. I knew that Stephen and Renae would be arriving some time that weekend, and Henry Harris, a longtime camp member who was a bit younger than me, was waiting at his lady friend's house over in Mount Union. I went outside to start unpacking, and recalling the sight of the old men still in their bunks, I began to reminisce about the many nights that my son and I had slept in this old, red, converted school bus that had become our weekend home away from home.

The Red Bus Sleeps

Here I lay, bottom bunk
eye-level with the yellow piss bucket.
Covers pulled over my head
as a first line of defense
from the mosquitoes who
never seem to bother the old men
only me, the youngest, too young
to have acquired all the secrets
of the Red Bus.

Each of the old men
is in bed performing his nightly rituals.
Revere nurses the juice out of
his moist tobacco leaves.
Fields is peeling and gnawing
his kielbasa into a masterpiece.
My father pulls his sweat hood

over his head, and waits for the
number dreams to come to him again.
And Mr. Bill, always the first asleep,
rests wisely in the big bed. The bed
that I could only sheepishly steal moments in
when Mr. Bill was out fixing an un-noticeable
part of the Red Bus.

Soon after time had given
us a piece of sleep out of her purse,
Uncle Nash would return from the Elks.
Instinct would undress him, and
he would stumble back toward the piss bucket,
step in some of Revere's spit, and the festivities
would begin;
"Goddamn it Revere, why the hell you don go
and spit that shit on the floor? What the hell
kind of sense that make?"
Revere half asleep replied; "Shit on you Nash, I'm asleep."
Fields stirred, "Damn it Nash, folks is trying to sleep."
Then as only my Uncle Nash could respond,
"You wasn't trying to sleep when I caught you
with that ugly girl in '47, so why you trying to sleep now?"
I tried to muffle my giggles, the numbers
kept my father's ears shut, and Mr. Bill
just slept soundly.

Uncle Nash argued on while he began to piss.
I moved closer to the wall in preparation
for the ensuing drunken concerto.
It started with a drum solo into the bucket,
then a melody from the carpet as he swayed.
Next the frame of my bed would chime in briefly
before the harmonic pelting on my bedspread.
Finally back to the bucket, the piss drumming

kept time with the argument. As the music
was coming to its climax, Mr. Bill stirred;
"Y'all shut the hell up. Shit."
His voice was only a slight murmur
well below the tone of the chaos.
We all were sure that we heard him saying something
but no one dared postulate what and
the possibility of what he might have said
left us all silent. Suddenly Uncle Nash went back to
his bed, and before he could lay down, Revere
and Fields were already snoring. It was as if
they somehow knew what he must have said and responded,
but I, the youngest, sat up wondering, wishing
I too was old, and could understand

Mama often said, "It takes a lot of living to make a house a home." For
more than twenty years, Omari and I, along with our old fishing buddies,
made the Red Bus home. We lived there during most of the weekends in
May, June, and July, as well as when we took several three- and four-day
fishing trips in August. By the time that Omari had reached manhood,
we fishermen had become an extended family with many ties that
bound us into a very closely knit group.

In addition to Uncles Nash and William, the other regular camp
members were several retired steel mill workers and a few other guys
from Johnstown and Mount Union. Mr. Revere was a fishing sensation,
and could out-fish most of the older guys. During our camp's fishing contests, it usually took Henry Harris, Omari, or me, the youngest members,
to put him in check. Mr. Thomas could hold his own when it came to
fishing for big bass, but he preferred drifting in a boat to wading the river
with the rest of us. Sam Fields constantly spat tobacco juice as he sat on
the bank in Kistler, only periodically catching fish. Because he had "Old
Arthur" in his knees, Mr. Fields seldom waded the river. No one loved
to eat the fresh fish more than Sammie Johnson, although he seldom

had the patience to catch them. The feistiest old man for his age was Old Man George Johnson, even though it took two of us to help him walk down to the river and get situated. When it was time to leave, we put a rope around his waist, and one of us used the rope to pull him up, while a second person walked behind him, with their hands supporting his back as he went up the riverbank. In his late eighties, he was still the most trash-talking old man I knew.

Old Man George Johnson always kept a pistol on his side because he said that he had to be ready for snakes and "redneck crackers," both of whom he claimed had a "tendency to break bad." In all the time we fished together, he never shot at either. Even though he could hardly walk, and one stiff drag on the wine bottle made him high, he insisted, "I can drink all the liquor I want," and bragged, "Boy, I'll skin my peter on any young gal I can catch." Once he told me, "Son, age ain't got nothing to do with me. I'm from the old school. Color don't too much matter to me either. If you don't believe me, you just bring me one of them high yaller gals down here. Or, you can bring me one of them white stringy-haired hillbillies or a young sassy black gal from up town — it don't make no difference to me. I'll tear her ass up!"

As I laughed, Uncle William, who loved to tease Old Man George Johnson, yelled, "Shut up Johnson. You know your dick won't salute no more. What the hell you gonna do with a young gal? You can't do any good with an old woman, much less a young gal. And you better not let Ms. Mamie hear you talking all that shit."

Fully in command of his wit, Johnson came right back. "If you believe that Bill, then you bend your naked ass over in front of me. Then we'll see what I can and can't do. You just come on over here. I'll have you screaming like a billy goat."

As Uncle William and I rolled with laughter, Uncle William slipped on the muddy bank, and fell flat on his butt. Old Man George Johnson chimed in again, "See you wouldn't bring it to me, and now you done fell on that big butter butt of yours, Bill."

Henry Harris, small in stature with natural blond hair, was the best fisherman from Mount Union. Although we worried about his clogged arteries, Henry Harris took his prescribed heart medicine in between shots of Canadian blended whiskey, rum, or whatever was his current drink of choice; he and a friend could drink a fifth while cutting the grass around the bus. He did care enough about his health not to eat cheeseburgers when Omari and I decided to cook them. According to Henry Harris, whiskey cleaned his arteries, and cheeseburgers clogged them. Drinking or not, there was no one who systematically out-fished Henry Harris, and there was no finer gentleman. Over the years, Henry Harris became my closest camp friend, aside from my relatives.

My brother Stephen had been a regular camp member throughout his college days, and I was especially glad that he, too, was coming this weekend. After he got married, both he and his wife would drive their trailer up to camp three or four times a year. When God called Stephen to preach, his fishing got curtailed, eventually being reduced to our annual Memorial Day weekend trip, an occasional Saturday, or a weekend when he got "excused from the pulpit" on the fifth Sunday of a summer month. Stephen was eleven years younger than I and, because I spent so much time teaching and caring for him while fishing, as well as throughout his college years, he became more like my son and eventually my closest friend than my brother. We knew each other's fishing styles and habits so well that we could spend hours on the river without talking, other than to compliment a nice catch. Stephen was also very athletic, and with him at my side, I was comfortable wading into much deeper water than I would wade with the older men or a young child like Omari. We grew so close that, years later, I often called Omari "Stephen" when only Omari and I were fishing.

Camp "membership" was confirmed with annual dues that began at twenty-five dollars and gradually went up to fifty dollars over the years. I always paid more to help with Uncle William's many repairs of the bus. One "member" was a very senior citizen who never paid his dues. We put up with him not paying because he loved to fish so much and we all enjoyed his love of fishing, but he was the object of many jokes related to giving his money, fish, and other possessions to young women for sexual favors. Moreover, not paying was something that he and only he could get away with, and thus he had an acknowledged "bad nigger" attitude that we all liked without saying so. It was much more fun complaining to each other, and periodically asking him when he planned to pay his dues.

For many unforgettable years, we fished, cooked, ate, shared life experiences, relaxed, and enjoyed the experience of each other's company; this was all made possible by Uncle William's decision to remodel an old yellow school bus back in 1970. He stripped the bus of its seats, installed six bunk beds, a table, sink, front and rear electric lights, a refrigerator, and a heater. He painted it the color of a red barn, adding a black stripe down each side. The remodeling task completed, Uncle William registered the bus in his name with the Bureau of Motor Vehicles, and drove it to our campground in the little borough of Kistler, across from the Juniata River.

In addition to six bunk beds, Uncle William installed one floor-level, regular-sized bed for himself. No one ever slept in that bed but Uncle William, even when he was not there. To produce customized mattresses for the bunk beds, Uncle William cut larger mattresses in sections, and sewed pieces to fit. During grade school, Omari used a bottom bunk for safety reasons. Later, upon arriving at camp, he always put his sleeping blanket on the top bunk in the middle of the bus. The oldest fishermen preferred to sleep on the bottom where they would not risk injuries associated with rolling out of the top bunks after too much to drink, and it was easier for them to get up during the night to use the piss bucket. Sleeping in a lower bunk also helped Mr. Fields spit his tobacco juice into his coffee can. After several summers, we ceased to be amazed by, but could never figure out how, Mr. Fields could simultaneously chew tobacco, eat cold kielbasa, and talk sporadically, all while lying down.

I always unrolled my sleeping bag on my "assigned" space (in the unspoken order of things), which was the bottom bunk in the rear of the bus where the door remained cracked all night. Back there, I was at first risk to an intruder (there never was one) and drafts on a cold summer night (there were plenty). After some of the oldest men quit coming to camp, I moved to the lower bunk in the front of the bus, and a younger camp member used my old bunk. Year after year, we used the same mattresses and eventually knew just how to position our bodies for a good night's sleep in their well-worn hollows. It bothered no one that Uncle Nash and/or Henry Harris washed the white sheets and pillow cases only once a year, or that over the years they turned gray with irregular brown spots.

On the small, blue, Formica-topped table inside the bus, I put all of my cooking supplies. Four people could sit uncomfortably around it, and in addition to dining, it served as a card table, a minibar, and a place for late tales of the day's fishing heroics. Above the table, two five-inch-wide boards served as shelves for everything from an assortment of preparations for the older men's various afflictions to tools, matches, playing cards, paper cups, and Louisiana Hot Sauce.

In the front of the bus, on the left as you entered, Uncle William had installed a sink with cold running water, and to its right, a bottled-gas stove. To the right of the oven, and just before Uncle William's personal bed, a dull, gray, antique-looking "china cabinet" held dishes and silverware purchased from a Goodwill store. A white-fading-to-yellow, second-hand refrigerator droned on and on throughout the year, chilling our catches, the "cold ones," and Omari's chocolate milk.

Inside and outside the bus, there were spiderweb-like electric cords running everywhere. One cord connected to an interior ultraviolet bug light, the zapping of which went on all through the night; falling to sleep amidst the crackling sounds of bugs being electrocuted was a fair trade-off to being bitten by the hungry mosquitoes. A brown cord was connected to a radio that sat outside year-round and brought in a local station, Magic 99, loud and clear. A black cord connected to a light over the sink. One had to be especially careful with this one. It had three separate cords going into it and their copper wires were partially exposed; making a connection with a wet hand resulted in a shock. I kept complaining that the wires had to be taped, but Uncle William insisted that it was nothing to worry about since, "that little bit of juice couldn't hurt a flea." Eventually, I taped the wires myself.

Outside, two lights hung over the twelve-foot, galvanized tin–covered table on which we cleaned fish, cooked, ate meals, and played cards on hot summer nights. There were cords connected to a fan, a second refrigerator, and a "Silver Bullet" neon beer sign on top of the bus. A thick, heavy-duty, black cord ran on the ground through the brush for about fifty yards, and connected to a box on a telephone pole. Only the veteran camp members knew to what most of the electric cords were connected, and only Uncle William understood all of the wiring. When a repair was needed, sometimes even Uncle William didn't understand the network of electrical wires, giving the rest of us good cause to worry. If Uncle William made a mistake—what he called a "miscue"—then one of us was likely to pay a price.

On two occasions, I directly experienced the results of Uncle William's electrical miscues. The first time was when I returned to camp, wet from the waist down. I kicked off my boots, and proceeded up the metal bus steps wearing my wet socks. After the electricity surged through my body, I jumped from the first step to the second, and from the second step to the top, and then back out of the bus. When the electricity hit me, things got gray and dreary, and warm water suddenly appeared in my pants.

Partially in panic and wanting to warn my son, I cried, "Holy shit! There's electricity everywhere. Omari, stand back!" Angered by the fact that Omari was laughing, I asked, "What in the hell do you think is so funny? I could have been killed!" Still laughing, he answered, "You should've seen your face and how you jumped." Walking ever so slowly as he came around the corner of the bus, Uncle William asked, "What happened, Jack Lee?" Bothered by his calm demeanor, I snapped, "I don't know what happened, but I do know that this damn bus is full of electricity." Still acting in what I thought to be too calm a fashion, Uncle William replied, "Hell, son. All it is is some sort of miscue. Let me check, and I'll have it fixed in a minute."

After tinkering with various electric wires, Uncle William declared, "See, I just forgot to fix the ground wire after I ran a new wire to the oil furnace. Go on in the bus. It wasn't nothing but a little miscue. I've straightened the damn thing out."

Not wanting to appear weak in front of Omari, and not wanting to show a lack of confidence in Uncle William's work, I put on my tennis shoes and ventured into the bus. It was a tremendous relief when nothing happened. With a broad smile on his face, Uncle William exclaimed triumphantly, "See, I told you boy. You always worrying about the wrong thing. Just trust your old uncle."

I experienced the second of Uncle William's miscues about a year later, when I grabbed the metal knob to turn on the outside water faucet. The jolt to my hand reminded me of the toy used to give someone a buzz during a handshake, though the effect was many times worse. Again, Uncle William showed no concern for me, and merely said, "Damn, I must have mis-wired that son of a bitch again." Thereafter, Omari always permitted me to be the one to make the initial contact with the metallic parts of the bus, turn the lights on when we first got to camp, and in general be the first to test for miscues.

When we arrived before everyone else during the early spring, I also checked the furnace because temperatures would sometime drop down into the low fifties at night. On such chilly nights, we had to make a choice between being cold or being warm but having the bus fill up with residual oil fumes and fearing a possible explosion. Until you fell into a deep sleep, you were awakened with each loud click of the furnace cutting off and on during the night. Some nights, we elected to be cold. It was such a relief to get to camp and find that Uncle William already had everything functioning properly.

The bus offered only a "piss bucket" inside for those too old or without the will to go outside during the night. We had a traditional outhouse in which a conventional toilet stool had been placed. A person could carry water, pour it into the tank, and flush the toilet one time. If you used it, you had to take your turn cleaning that toilet. Most of us, therefore, used the woods behind the bus. Because those woods were also where we buried fish guts, were full of poison ivy, and at night were full of real and imagined wild things, Omari "held it" until he could find a toilet somewhere in town. Uncle William had real class, and he always used the fully furnished toilet, taking great delight in its ability to flush outdoors. Hearing the flush of an outdoor toilet caused everyone to laugh, especially the first time one heard it.

This particular Friday morning, after completing my inspection inside the bus and chatting with the old men, I went outside to the all-purpose table, which stood under a metal roof supported by posts made from nearby trees. The first year that we built the roof over the table, leaves remained on the posts throughout the summer. The lean-to roof was covered with tin, which was covered in turn with carpeting to soften the sound of the rain and to ward off the sun's heat. The entire outdoor area was enclosed with screens to keep out insects and small animals. When we sat outside at night, we lit damp rags so that the smoke also repelled insects. Before going fishing, I cleared the table of the empty bottles, cans, and old newspapers used to make a tablecloth, and then spread new newspaper and sat out my cooking supplies so that they would be ready when we got back from fishing and wanted to relax.

Omari was growing impatient, and since it was going on eight in the morning and Stephen had not arrived, I decided to leave. The other guys were still in bed, and so I left Stephen a note as to where he'd find us—a place he and I had discovered years ago.

Going down the path behind the old Mennonite church, pine needles covered the ground and everywhere there were signs of early spring growth. Poison ivy was in abundance and the freshly hatched flies made me wish I was wearing a bee mask. We made our way along the ancient path, to the big bend in the river where we always began to fish. In less than an hour, Omari and I each had more than twenty beautiful rock bass that were about seven inches long and wider than the palm of my hand. I couldn't wait to show them off at camp. We continued downstream, fishing, enjoying the isolation and a flock of wild ducks that was swimming on the other side. As the sun was fully overhead and it was approaching noon, we decided to quit fishing, and with our stringers loaded with fish, we headed back up the hill, slipping and sliding as we made our way through damp weeds, weighted down by the fish. By the time we got back to my car, we were putting seventy-three fish on ice. We decided to go back to the camp, since Stephen hadn't caught up with us, and we figured he might be back there.

Omari gave the blow-by-blow of our morning catch as I got the paper plates, napkins, hot sauce, mustard, ketchup, and bread from inside the bus. He ended by going to the car, getting a stringer of lunker rock bass out of the ice chest, and holding them up for everyone to see. Uncle William smiled and kept frying fish. Almost two hours and three hot fish sandwiches apiece later, we loaded three cars and headed for Lewistown where we put on one of our fishing contests through the rest of the afternoon. Omari took great pleasure in besting me and was cocksure that he would win the pot of fifty cents apiece to which we had all contributed. It gave me some source of satisfaction when later, back at the camp, Mr. Revere reached into his ice chest, laid a true trophy wild brown trout on the metal-topped table, and inquired, "You all want to give me your money now or later?" Omari needed to remember that though he was good, he was fishing with the best.

It was close to nine-thirty at night when everybody finished cleaning their catch. After the full day on the river, sitting around camp talking, eating, and drinking late into the night was the perfect ending to a beautiful day. All of the exaggerated stories and humorous lies reminded me of the "lying contests" that Zora Neale Hurston wrote about in *Mules and Men*. I was glad Omari was there listening to the stories, experiencing alternative models of African American male behavior. I believed that a young male child needed to see contrasting male roles. I perceived my father as the faithful husband, reliable deacon, hard worker, and responsible Masonic leader, and at the same time, saw my two hero uncles drink heavily, love hard, work hard, treat their children as well as Daddy treated us, and in general have a good time, or as they said, "live the life." I also wanted the fishing camp socialization process to prevent Omari from going down the African American, middle-class, nerd highway that was possible while living in an upper-class, suburban neighborhood like ours. Life at the Red Bus was about as much of a culture contrast as Omari could get from his day-to-day existence at this point in his life.

For more than two decades, three generations of African American men gathered here, and from their substantive interactions built enduring relationships. Within and around that bus, the oldest connected with the youngest. Being in the middle, I learned from the oldest as well as the youngest and sometimes served as a bridge between the two. Fishing in pairs, Henry Harris was as much a son to Uncle Nash as Omari was to me. Uncle William loved taking Old Man George Johnson fishing during the years when Ms. Johnson trusted no one else to take her aging husband on the river. Feeling good about all of the attachments we formed over the years, and being really pleased with how well the day had gone, I regretted only that Stephen was not present. I knew preaching was something I should not question, but why couldn't God provide him with more time for fishing—more time for me to renew and enjoy my close ties with my brother? I went to bed that night missing him and the times we spent together on the river, but I fell asleep reflecting on more pleasant thoughts of how well Omari had mastered fishing the big river.

MR. BILL

SIX-THIRTY the next morning seemed to have come only a few minutes after I had slipped into deep sleep. From below my half-drawn, faded cream window shade, I caught a glimpse of a rising yellow-orange sun, indicating the coming of another warm and wonderful fishing day. The slow throb in my head increased as the sunrise penetrated my eyes, and I became aware of the fact that last night I had kept company with Mr. Gordon's Gin longer than I had thought was the case. Closing my eyes to relax, I laid there thinking about the best possible places to fish. About fifteen minutes later, I reached over and awakened Omari by gently tugging at his covers. We took about fifteen more minutes to get ourselves together, and then got dressed, brushed our teeth, briefly washed our faces with cold water, and headed to the car.

While I was moving slowly and loading the trunk, Stephen and Renae pulled into camp. Their presence lifted my spirits, and I yelled, "Get your equipment, and put it in my car! You don't need to bring your bait. I have enough for everyone." Omari looked at me as if to say, "There goes that fever again."

I really was very excited; today was going to be great. God had provided both the opportunity for Stephen to go fishing and excellent weather. Trying not to show too much emotion, I nevertheless jumped into my car, started the engine, pressed the gas pedal several times, and yelled again, "You all come on! I've never been this late in heading over to the river." After they laughed, finished loading in their gear, and climbed in the backseat, Renae asked, "Okay, where's the best place to go? Take us to where I can catch a few nice ones, some spot where you left a few fish in the river yesterday." With that, I sped off and, a few miles past a series of cornfields, turned onto a one-lane dirt road that led down to a huge sycamore tree overhanging the river. Below the tree, throughout a lengthy stretch of the river, there was a series of huge boulders and sunken trees around which fish always gathered. We quickly got into our gear and fanned out across the water, each seeking his or her favorite spot. Fishing throughout the morning in water over our waists, we slowly waded about a half-mile down the river, filling our stringers, two fish to a snap. Then the fully risen sun began to take its toll on me, causing a sense of dehydration, an ever increasing headache, and a strong desire to be sitting in the shade back at the camp. Noticing that Stephen and Renae had been in the same spot for a long time, I inquired, "You two about ready to head back and cook some fish?" Renae answered, "Anytime you are. We've caught enough fish, and remember, we got up real early this morning." Hearing that, I immediately called across the river to Omari, "Hey, let's go. Stephen and Renae are tired, and so we're heading back to camp."

We fished along the bank as we waited for Omari to join us and, when he did, I proudly held up my stringer and said, "Here, carry these heavy fish up this hillside for me." Poking fun, he answered, "Give me those tiny things," and then tossed them over his shoulder as I climbed up the riverbank. Saving time, I led the group straight up the hill, trampling the thick underbrush and clearing a path as I proceeded. We got back to the camp a few minutes past noon and spotted Uncle William sitting under the shed.

He had remained in camp to work on the oil furnace's motor, fixing something only he understood. When Omari and Stephen lifted our stringers out of the cooler, he yelled, "Where the hell you catch that many fish? Damn, we're going to have to keep the four of you out of the river. You've caught enough fish to open a fish market." I responded, "Well, you're going to think we're running a restaurant when Stephen and I start frying these fish. Omari, get my stringer of fish out to clean." Joining the banter, Omari offered, "Daddy, you don't have enough fish on that stringer of yours. I'd better get mine."

We all laughed and then set about cleaning Omari's fish. As I watched Uncle William work on the motor, I began to see more clearly his growing tendency to do small, "something to do" things around the camp rather than fish. Now he was tinkering with the motor, trying to make it run more smoothly and produce less noise when we slept. Thinking about how his various ailments had gradually taken him off the river, it seemed as though it hadn't been that long ago that Omari started fishing with his uncles and me. Yet, as Omari grew from a child in grade school to a young man, I went from being "in my prime" to what Jerri called "approaching membership in the over-the-hill gang." Along the way, we saw many of our fishing buddies grow too old to fish, turn to an assortment of medicines, and die. Some of us were merely "maturing," others were simply getting "up there," and no matter what euphemistic terms we used to describe our transitions, all of us were going somewhere in time. Thus, many of our late-night sitting-around-the-camp conversations were increasingly about life's transitions, particularly the sometimes-disturbing realities of aging. On many of those nights, Uncle Nash entertained us with his descriptions of aging's consequences.

The Road to Manhood Is Longer than It Seems

"Boy pray the Lord
takes you when you're young,
cause when you get old
you ain't worth a shit."

Immediately my father responded to Uncle Nash
like the child in grade school
who, rather than ponder the lesson
speaks from a wisdom clearly
wanting to be bested by experience.
"Well why are you still here?" he asked.

Uncle Nash too wise
to ever hesitate answered:
"I'm already here so I might as well stay,
but y'all are still young, and have time to pray."
Having reconfirmed the hierarchy
he rose in pain, and began to walk away,
the first step was more of a skillful hobble,
then those legs filled with pride
carried him assuredly along, with the sun
always respectfully at his back.

My father, now 50,
has been my main guide
in the quest for manhood.
But now he sits beside me
blind as me
learning from Uncle Nash.
It wasn't until then
as my father watched Uncle Nash go,
and he turned to grin at me,
saying, "Pray the Lord takes you while you're young."
that I knew the complete man I see in my father
is just another traveler a little closer to the end of the road.

Whereas Uncle Nash always complained about aging, Uncle William, "Mr. Bill" to others, aged silently like a good jug of rye-based, crystal clear "hard water" from the backwoods stills of Virginia. Slowly, however, we noticed Uncle William's aging more by what he didn't do at the camp. Because we depended on him so much for maintaining the Red Bus, my alert system went up a significant notch when he was not in camp; sometimes, I actually got jumpy, especially when Omari and my nephew Daniel were the only ones with me there. I had no idea of what to do if we suddenly lost our electricity, the old rusty lawn mower refused to start or the water line broke, but Mr. Bill was a living lesson in innovation and ingenuity. "Handyman" only begins to express his engineering genius. I often wondered what he would have been like if he had been given the opportunity to pursue an engineering degree.

His creative abilities were matched by his generosity to his many nieces and nephews. All of my cousins believed that he was such a mighty good man, that when God got around to creating uncles, he created Uncle William as the First Uncle. We remembered fondly how Uncle William always gave us money for snacks, bought clothes for some of us, advised most of us, sometimes served as a second father for many of us, socialized with us at family gatherings, and treated all of us as if we were his children. We never encountered Uncle William without him giving us something, whether it was a word of support or some material gift.

After being chastised by a parent, Uncle William could help you see the good that your parent's yelling, whipping, or other form of punishment had failed to make clear. Once, Mama whipped me for coming in after dark. I was fifteen years old, and all of my friends could stay out until ten and eleven at night. Uncle William came in as I sat crying in the kitchen, and asked, "What's wrong with you, Jack Lee?"

"Mama beat me because I came in late, and everybody else is still outside playing Tin Can Alley. I'm the only guy my age in the house."

"That may be true, but do all of your friends get enough to eat everyday? Do all of your friends know where their mamas are right now? Your mama just wants you to make something of yourself, grow up and be somebody. You can't do that running the streets all hours of the night. And your mama just wants the best for you, that's all."

I thought about how we teased Tyrone who lived with his oldest sister because he didn't know where his mother lived. Then my mood changed completely when Uncle William said, "Here, take this and buy yourself some ice cream tomorrow. See, you wouldn't have gotten this if you had been out in the street and missed me."

Uncle William was a man of so much integrity that he earned the name "Mr. Bill" from adults as well as children, and using his name was like a second passport for me. Just as "Deacon Daniel's son" was my "open sesame" for those who lived the strictly sacred life style, "Mr. Bill Young's nephew" had the same impact in the secular world as well as among many of the "saints." As Mr. Bill Young's nephew, without being a member, I could get into all of Johnstown's African American night-clubs. His name got me into the Coke Plant Club, even though I was underage at nineteen. In Mount Union, if I needed help from someone in the local African American community, I only needed to introduce myself as Mr. Bill Young's nephew. The fact that I was the nephew who fished with him made me even more acceptable. Once I was inside the private Mount Union Elks club, where the locals knew I was the "fishing nephew," I would hear things like, "Well, if you are Mr. Bill Young's nephew, you've got to be all right. There's no better man than Mr. Bill Young." Next came my free drinks, "out of respect for Mr. Bill."

For more years than I can remember, I enjoyed the status of being the nephew of the great Mr. Bill Young, his unending generosity, his extraordinary fishing skills, and the comforts stemming from his ingenuity at camp. But while we were cleaning fish that Friday and Saturday, I noticed the unusual height of the weeds around the perimeter of the camp-ground. A few curious vines had curled their tentacles around the front fender of the bus and were seeking to climb higher. Earlier, walking along the path to the woods, the blackberry vines sticking to my shirt let me know that they had not been cut back in some time. These and other signs told me that Mr. Bill was indeed in transition.

Throughout the summer, he often spent most of the week at camp, and by the time that we arrived on the weekend, Uncle William usually had the grassy area immediately surrounding the bus well manicured, along with the weeds on the path leading to the woods and the edges of the driveway. Now I could see a few weeds producing seeds and flowers in their tops. Just as the grass and weeds received less and less attention, other aspects of the camp's comforts began to fall apart.

When a storm blew the antenna down from the top of the bus, Uncle William decided that it wasn't "worth the effort to put another one back up there." No one else had the tools, will, or skill to remount the antenna. After almost ten years of zapping bugs at night, the blue light in the front of the bus succumbed, and Uncle William decided not to replace it, either. When I inquired about what "we" were going to do about the bug light, Uncle William told me, "That damn light made too goddamn much noise anyway, and besides, a few mosquito bites won't kill you young boys. Leave it out, and we'll sleep a little better." Yet I remembered how proud Uncle William was when he had first installed the light saying, "That light sure raises hell with those bugs, and it gives just enough light for those of us who have to get up at night to take a piss. Yes sir, that light makes all the difference in the world."

Gradually I saw other kinds of changes, too. For years, when we got up in the morning, Mr. Bill began the day by popping open a can of beer, and pouring part of it into "his" glass. He never used a paper cup; he had his own special barroom glass, which, like his bunk bed, no one else ever used. After the suds finished sliding down the sides of his glass, with one long, deliberate sip, he slowly drank the beer down, and exclaimed, "Ah boy!" Next came two generous shots of gin into the glass, and the rest was filled with beer until the suds again ran over the sides of the glass. Given that this was a "mixed drink," two or three long, slow swallows were necessary to finish it off. Having completed this morning ritual, he was now ready to go fishing, and by seven-thirty in the morning, Mr. Bill would be somewhere with us on the river, and he would have caught a nice bass or two.

The end of his morning "pick-me-up" seemed to have begun when he woke up in the bus one morning, and said softly,

"Jack Lee, hand me my medicine from off the shelf. I have that hurting in my chest again. The medicine should clear it up by the time we're ready to go fishing."

"Okay, but if you want to rest longer, stay here and we'll come back for you in a couple of hours."

"No, I'll be okay. Just give me time for this medicine to kick in."

So, the morning beer and gin cocktail gave way to a number of self-prescribed "tonics" to relieve Uncle William's self-diagnosed cases of "indigestion and heartburn." For a while, a little baking soda on his tongue was his most reliable remedy, but the chest pains persisted. He got another prescription, but took only an approximate dosage because it was not to be taken with alcohol, and even then he took the medicine only after the baking soda failed to ease his pains.

The reality of Mr. Bill not drinking was difficult for me to digest. Fine women treated well, fine cars driven fast, fine fishing on the big river, and fine liquor drunk generously were all part of the dynamic persona that I cherished for years. Mr. Bill would drink and play poker all night in Johnstown, get picked up by me and Stephen around five o'clock Saturday morning, fish until noon, and then take several long drinks out of a gin bottle in order to "knock the chill and dampness" out of his body. Other men got drunk and then wrecked cars, beat women, threw away their money, and slowly destroyed their lives. I never saw Uncle William drunk, although he drank enough to make most men drunk. With women, he was Mr. Generosity, and he managed his money with the same skills that he used to maintain our camp. Now I was becoming painfully aware of how much we depended on his skills, as he fixed fewer things and fished less often.

With admiration, I remembered how Uncle William would "fish hard" all day. At that time, nobody spent more time on the river. After he quit wading the river, for a while, Uncle William made use of a metal chair that he had welded together. He made the chair extra high, so that he could sit in about three feet of water, with his feet barely touching the river. Wearing his hip boots, he would wade out, set up his chair, and fish for an hour or so without getting wet. His wide-brimmed straw hat helped to protect him from the sun. This Friday and Saturday, he avoided getting in the water at all. As the days passed that summer, "going back to the camp early" soon turned into, "I believe that I'll skip going out with you this morning. It is a little too cool, and I'll wait until it warms up a bit." The warm parts of the day became "too hot to fish," and Uncle William began to settle for sitting on the bank for about an hour in the evening, after "things had cooled down some." Today, fixing the furnace motor had become his priority.

When discussing the hard times of the Depression and the general hard knocks of being Negro and poor, my parents and their friends often talked about "makin' a way outta no way." With what others deemed "nothing," they could make something useful, like when they turned dyed flour sacks into skirts, dandelions into wine, and wild polk salad and watercress into gourmet vegetable dishes. With grocery money limited to the most basic staples, Daddy took us into the woods to gather wild apples and berries, which Mama canned, and we had fruit throughout the year. Around the Red Bus, Uncle William was the ultimate innovator, problem solver, "Mr. Fix It Up." With his ability to perform mechanical miracles, he built our "mobile home" which could sleep six per night for the cost of enough electricity to supply one light bulb. Thus, he was an inspiration to all of us, demonstrating conclusively that complex problems were there simply to be solved. I was so glad that Omari got to see this master builder at work, and I wished more young African American males had had the same opportunity, because without it, they lost yet another opportunity for their self-esteem to be enhanced.

Sure, there was a need for the agenda I had pressed relentlessly upon Omari, the need for him, early on as a child, to learn well the "alphabets" of math, English, and various aesthetics. However, equal opportunity was clearly going to be a long time coming for those other than the best of the African American middle class. So there was still a need for young men to have the sustaining hope that comes from having the knowledge and skill of "makin' a way outta no way" as Mr. Bill so ably demonstrated. As Uncle William himself put it when I asked him about how he was able to build and fix so many things, "Belief, son, belief is half of the thing."

Without the sustaining force of Mr. Bill's positive belief in human possibilities, young African American men can't conceive of building the Red Buses they need in their lives. Instead, in the grasp of despair, they pursue false promises such as criminal activities. Traveling this path, even if they manage to elude death at an early age, they still find themselves entangled in the web of the criminal justice system. Alienation is felt widely. Hope is lost. Seeking to make a way out of the wrong way, blind selfishness leads to the destruction of self and others becoming normative. Mr. Bill's way was a matter of helping others, paving ways where there seemed to be no paths to tread, and there was a spirit of mutual sharing as evidenced by the first sign that he put in the bus, "Gentlemen, whatever you see, help yourself. Be sure to replace it when you leave." Mr. Bill was an extension of the African American church's moral fiber, yielding hope in the midst of despair and offering an abiding faith in the positive possibilities that could flow from righteous efforts.

TRASH TALKING

White Flesh Underneath

We sat in the May sun scaling
the Memorial Day rock bass.
Our machine was in full gear,
Uncle Nash and I popping the
scales off, Uncle Steve slicing
the smaller fish open, passing
over the larger ones, which
my father would filet.

Henry Harris washed the fish,
separating the guts
from the meat, and Mr. Bill
the oldest, bagged them up.
The machine lumbered on,
the scraping of their flesh
sent the scales into the air.
Exposing the white flesh
underneath.

The scales settled randomly
attaching themselves to our
bodies, hardened and
became part of us.
The knives piercing their
heads sent streams of
blood off the table into
the gray pebbles below.

There were the sounds
of tiny balloons popping
each time the filet knife
struck a lung.
Uncle Steve's
knife scratched the metal
table like fingernails
with each
head he removed.

The stripped
carcasses were flung into a
bloody bucket.
Each body
sloshed on top of the next,
reminding me of the sound
boots make when walking
in thick mud.
The white meat
made belly smackers
into the pans of water,
where they awaited
the washing and bagging.
The sweat made our
black skin glisten in the May sun.

WE HAD so many fish to clean that Uncle William decided to help us. Omari, Stephen, Renae, and I already had one five-gallon bucket brimming with fish heads and guts, including yellow sacks of eggs that began to smell shortly after being removed. Another water bucket was almost half full with scales and gray slime wiped from the table by those scaling. While filleting, I had twice cut my left thumb. The second cut caused a five-minute delay while I stopped the bleeding. After tying a strip of cloth around it, I continued filleting. Lying on the ground were several more stringers of fish.

When Uncle William joined us, trying to encourage the others, I said, "Good, now we can clean all of these fish, get rid of this garbage, wash the table down, and get ready for a fish fry." Stephen looked at the fish on the ground, sat his scaler down, flexed his fingers, and then said, "Sounds good to me." Renae seized the opportunity and said with a smile, "Okay, you men go on and finish the job. I'm going to clean up and relax until lunch is served."

After scaling about five fish, Uncle William complained, "My hands are cramping up on me. Plus, it has gotten too damn hot for me to do much of anything. Y'all go ahead and clean the rest of them. I'm going to have myself a Coke, and lay back on this reclining chair a minute or two until the rest of the boys get back." I knew what he meant; he had decided, as my kids would say, to "chill." Unless it got nice and cool during the late evening, and we decided to fish down by the Brickyard or the Blind Man Camp where he loved to sit on the bank and "hang a few big fish," Uncle William was going to be "chilling" for the rest of the day.

A few minutes after Uncle William had kicked back with his Coke, Uncle Nash pulled in with a car full of fishermen. After everyone got out of the car, Uncle Nash leaned out of his window and yelled to me, "Jack Lee, cook my fish last! I'm going to run over there to see Sally. I'll be back in about an hour, after I have a drink or two with her. I promised to bring her a few fish." Everyone knew that Uncle Nash hated to clean fish, and so Henry Harris said jokingly, "Mr. Nash, that woman ain't thinking about your old ugly ass. Stay here and help clean these fish. You had your fun catching them, now help us clean them." As he was turning his car around, Uncle Nash answered, "Henry, all these other guys can help. I'll be right back. Just because Josie don't want your little red ass don't mean Sally ain't waiting to see me." Then he spun the wheels of his car on the gravel, swerved out into the road, and sped off, leaving a trail of dust.

Like his Uncle Nash, Omari didn't then and still doesn't like to clean fish. Throughout grade school, Omari's desire to have nothing to do with cleaning made his "assistance" quite limited, but, at camp, everyone had to help in some way. Most of the time, I assigned him the tasks of getting water, washing the fish once they were scaled and gutted, putting them in plastic bags and then on ice, and handing the rest of us drinks. Eventually, he moved up to scaling, and became one of the best in the camp.

There were good reasons for not wanting to clean fish. Omari and I generally returned to camp with between seventy-five and one hundred fish a day. Scaling, gutting, rinsing, filleting and storing the fish required more than an hour's work. In May, even though we worked in a screened-in area, we still had to contend with the hatches of flies. Mosquitoes were always around during the evening, and in July and August, yellowjackets flew over your head, landing periodically on the bucket of fish guts or the scaled fish lying on the table. In addition, few things were as painful as dragging a scaler across your thumb and peeling back your skin instead of fish scales. As your thumb throbbed, several of your other fingers and the palm of your hand would be stinging from the innumerable times fish fins had stuck you when you caught them and now as you handled them. Then came a puncture or two from the tip of the knife when you stuck it through the side of the fish, and, because it was so sharp, the knife tip ran out the other side and into your hand. Fifty or sixty fish later, your hands were swollen from the various wounds. More often than I can recall, I had to put the knife down and take a drink of whatever the guys had open at the time. Fillet gloves could be used, but by the tenth fish or so, there was so much slime on them that the fish slipped, which slowed the cleaning process.

After the cleaning, five-gallon buckets of guts, heads, scales, fins, and carcasses were buried in holes behind the camp where we probably had the most fertile fifty square yards in the county. I often told Omari it was time for him to play grave digger by preparing several two- to three-foot-deep holes for burying the fish remains. Every now and then, some deviant simply threw the fish guts into the woods, and the high summer temperatures caused the funky stench of the rotting, maggot-filled meat to last nearly a week. Everyone denied having any knowledge of this, and Uncle William usually threatened, "I'm going to throw somebody's god-damn ass out of the camp. Don't let me find out who did that shit." Sometimes when only Omari and I were in camp, and he was too young to be of much assistance in cleaning the fish, my hands would get so sore I did throw fish guts into the woods without burying them. Even then, I only did so on the last day of camp when I knew the raccoons would eat most of it overnight, and within a few days, the heavy spring rains would rinse away the odor.

We took tremendous pride in what we did with those knives and scalers as thousands of fish got cleaned during our years of gathering at the camp. One learned the importance of having good tools, keeping the knives razor sharp, knowing how to pace your scaling with the speed at which the other person worked with the knife, and, indirectly, the benefits of being skilled and productive people.

In addition, we had to make decisions on how to prepare the fish depending on how they were to be used and to whom we were giving them. The largest fish served as "stuffers." These we left the heads on, and slit open their bellies to form pockets into which one could stuff crabmeat before the fish were broiled or baked at home.

Mrs. Pace never wanted me to bring her fish with the heads on them, claiming, "Son, with them heads on them like that, the fish seem like they're looking up at me from the dead. I don't want the dead looking at me till I'm dead." On the other hand, Mrs. Martin wanted them left on because she used the heads to make flavoring for what she called "South Carolina fish stew." Daddy wanted the heads cut off the smallest fish, but asked us to leave the fins on the fish. After the fish were fried, he used the fins to pull out many of the bones. He claimed that the smallest fish tasted the best, but after his eyes got bad, also admitted that he could fry the small fish real crispy, pull the fins to get out most of the bones, and just chew up the rest of the fish bones with his false teeth.

Until she was about eighty, Mama didn't want fillets because, "the fish seem to taste so much better when they're fried and picked off the bones," although when her eyesight also started to fail, we had to start bringing her fillets and one or two of what she called "those big long ones that I can see how to pick." Marijata always placed her order for some fillets, and Jerri loved the "stuffers." Every Mother's Day weekend Omari and I each caught one for her. Regardless of how people wanted their fish prepared, everyone agreed there was nothing better than those fresh fish we gave them.

Omari never stopped eating only fillets; I began preparing his fish that way when he was too young to pick bones. I ate fillets with Omari, but at camp, preferred picking the bones while talking with the older men who never filleted fish. For them, a vital part of the camp experience was sitting around, drinking, and savoring every morsel of fish as they slowly picked the bones and talked plenty of trash.

Even though our camp conversations were often pretty raunchy, I was glad that Omari was there. Just as Daddy and Mama thought it would do their three oldest sons some good to spend their summers working on the farm in Virginia, I thought it would do Omari some good to be exposed to the more secular dimensions of African American men like his great uncles. William and Nash were my ultimate role models for African American, working-class men who knew how to "make long money" and "live the good life." I was always enamored by their new cars, which they constantly drove beyond the speed limits. They were the "teasing-tan," greased-down-wavy-haired, fashionable suit-wearing men who knew how to relate to women and liquor. They slaved away in the steel mills of Johnstown, and then they partied longer than everyone. Even though they lived fast and free, they also had widely held reputations for being really decent men with a strong sense of commitment to family members and other loved ones. Watching them, I grew up determined to get my share of what seemed to me to be the products of that "good life."

I also loved the way my two uncles could "talk trash," which they did plenty of around the bus at night. They told hysterically funny stories, and engaged in those debates that customarily occur in male enclaves. Sitting in his ringside seat, I thought Omari would learn some down-to-earth things that would supplement what I and other middle-class males had to offer him. By the time a fishing weekend was over, Omari usually returned home having gotten an earful.

One night at camp, Uncle William reminisced, "Years ago, when I was a young man, I got paid and went to see one hell of a woman. I'd cashed my check, and had every cent in my pocket. After that big, blackberry-colored, fine-legged gal opened the door, I stepped inside and threw all of my money into the air. You should've seen the look on her face when I said, 'Baby, everything that stays up in the air is mine. All that falls on the ground is yours.' Man, that gal began to hug and kiss me, and then she picked up the money and handed it back to me. She thought I was playing, but I meant every word of what I said. From then on, every time she saw me, she yelled, 'Here comes my money man.' God, that woman loved me."

Uncle William often started the discussions of contemporary public issues. One Saturday at lunchtime, faking total naivete, he asked, "Henry, what the hell is the AIDS?" Henry took a big swallow of beer, laughed, and answered, "I don't know for sure, Mr. Bill, but they say that somehow it fucks up your immune system or something like that. You get sick as hell, and die. Ask your nephew. He has a doctor's degree."

Before I could say anything, Uncle William replied, "Dying ain't nothing to me Henry. At my age, I'm dying anyway. My heart or something might give out on me before the AIDS would have time to kill me. They say that little Jamison girl with the big, fine ass has the AIDS. But if she offers me some of that pussy, I'm gonna get them damned AIDS."

At this point, I cautioned jokingly, "I don't know, Uncle William. From what they say, if you see that Jamison girl, you had better head in the opposite direction. She might be pretty, but no sex is worth dying over." Wanting to keep things going, and shifting just a little, he commented on my education, adding, "See, I told you before. You got too much of that damn college education. I believe that doctor's degree of yours has you messed up, boy. That's what makes you say shit like that. Now me, if she comes my way, I'm just going to have to get the AIDS. You know you would do the same thing. You just talking shit because your son is sitting here."

Uncle Nash couldn't resist an opportunity to stir things up a bit by stating, "Aw hell, Bill. What you gonna do with your old ass? Use your tongue on that young girl?" Rising to that challenge, Uncle William came back with, "Don't you worry, Nash. What the hell you been doing with Ms. Sally? That's why I don't drink out of any glass that you use. I don't know where in the hell your lips have been. You got back here mighty quick today. So you must have used your lips instead of your hips. You certainly weren't tired when you got back here."

I mused aloud with false wonder, "I always wondered why you always used your own glass, Uncle William. Now I know." Looking at me as if I didn't pose a sufficient challenge to him, Uncle Nash just laughed. The discussion got defused when we shifted to who had caught what so far that day.

As we pressed on with cleaning the fish and preparing them for cooking, seemingly from nowhere, Mr. Stevenson asked, "Jack Lee, didn't you have more than the limit yesterday? You cleaned an awful lot of fish."

"No, why would I keep more than the limit?"

"Because you don't know when to stop. I believe you were over the limit, and if you keep on, you're going straight to hell for stuff like that."

Before I could answer, seeming like a disturbed man in the middle of a bad dream, Uncle Nash sat his beer down and speaking quite loudly, almost yelling, he held forth about God, Jesus, hell, and the situation of African Americans.

"I'm sick and tired of hearing niggers talk about dying and going to hell. After all that the white man has done to us on earth, I don't believe there's such a thing as hell other than right here. And if there is a hell, what kind of God would send any nigger to hell after all the hell niggers have caught right here in Johnstown, Conemaugh, Mount Union, Virginia, and everywhere else in this damn country?"

Once Uncle Nash got started, someone would always push him further with his favorite "sermon." All that was necessary this time was for Henry Harris to say, "You're being kind of hard on God. God could be listening to all that trash you're talking, and strike your ass dead right now. We'll be hauling your ass to the funeral parlor instead of eating lunch. Besides, we have a preacher sitting here, and you ought not talk that way in front of him."

Continuing in the same loud, complaining voice, Uncle Nash answered, "I'll talk any damn way I want to in front of my nephew, Steve, especially with Steve's wife over there in that trailer with the door shut. I knew Steve since he was a baby. How the hell did some God let white people do to my people what they did down in Virginia? The white man worked us all damn day for next to nothing. White folks would kill a nigger, tie a rope around his neck, and drag his body all through the streets. Where the hell was God when they was cutting off niggers' private parts, and hanging them in those damn trees? Where was God then? You ask Reverend Steve Daniel about that. Tell me, where was God when niggers needed him? Motherfuck a God if he is going to let that kind of shit go on!

"Everywhere you go, black people or colored people or whatever you want to call them are catching hell, and you going to talk to me about some God? Damn that! Where in the hell is hell if hell ain't right here? Shit, niggers are crazy talking about, 'I ain't going to do this' and 'I ain't going to do that cause God will put me in hell.' I don't believe all that dumb shit. Put me in hell! Where the hell was God when those white men took that goddamn stick and stuck it up my grandmother, and made her bleed? Don't try to tell me about some God going to do this, and some God is going to do that to me when I die, and he let that shit happen. When God let something like that happen to my grandmother, I say, Motherfuck a God! Jack Lee, you have the damn doctor's degree. You tell me, what kind of God is that who would pull so much shit on niggers?"

Knowing that Omari was listening, but not knowing how he was reacting and cautious with my own view of God, I tried to be judicious by saying, "I don't know, Uncle Nash. After all we've been through, somebody does need to give us an explanation. You know the Bible says God helps those who help themselves, so I spend my time at work trying to create more ways to help ourselves. But I came up here to fish; I'll let you figure out what God is up to. Now I want to get ready to eat lunch."

He was on a roll though, and his liquor, as well as our listening rather than ignoring, was facilitating his rapid tongue. He lashed out with, "Figure out my ass. Like Bill said, you've got too much education to know any damn thing. I know what God is up to with my people. God put our asses right in hell—right here in Johnstown, working ourselves to death for next to nothing at the Bethlehem Steel Coke plant, and letting all of the white men be the bosses, whether they had the education or not. Back then, we niggers worked like dogs all day for next to nothing. I just don't see how niggers can talk that foolishness about heaven and hell. I've seen all the hell I'm ever going to see, and if God can be that rotten to send me to another hell on top of this hell I have already lived, then shame on a God like that. To hell with that shit. I ain't that big of a fool."

Gently, Uncle William said, "Come on, Nash, stop all of that ugly talk. Jack Lee's son is sitting here and listening to everything you are saying. You ought to stop that stuff. Just like Jack Lee told you, these boys came up here to go fishing and have their fun eating a few fresh fish. They don't want to hear all of your trash."

Nash always listened to Uncle William. The two of them were much more than blood relatives; they were brothers, fishing and hunting buddies, and lifelong best friends. I never saw two men have greater respect for each other. They shared cars, good and bad times, money, homes, food, clothing, and truly did whatever they could do for one another. They were soul mates, and based on those bonds, Uncle William was the only one in camp who could get him to stop condemning God to hell. Stephen's being a preacher meant nothing as far as his ability to say anything to Uncle Nash about God; as far as Nash was concerned, the uncle to nephew relationship outweighed whatever relationship Stephen had with God.

Long before Uncle William was able to end the sermon, the rest of us had shut up. No matter how many times you had heard "Motherfuck a God," each live rendition was scarier than the last. Omari and my nephew Daniel often sat bug-eyed, waiting for God to hurl the largest thunderbolt possible into the bus. The older men sat in silence, fearing the potential wrath of God as well as the possibility that Uncle Nash might accuse them of being some of the specific "God-believing dumb niggers" he was talking about.

One May night, two years earlier, there had been a tremendous thunderstorm during one of his rants. Thunder seemed to be bouncing off the metal walls, and the lightning lit up the whole inside of the bus. I expected all of us to be consumed by one giant fireball when a lightning bolt struck the oil tank on the side of the bus. That night, I steadied myself by taking another stiff drink of gin. Then, I tried an oblique move to silence Uncle Nash by offering him a drink, but he just took a drink out of the bottle, swallowed it in one gulp, and went back into the same rant.

Mr. Revere timidly complained, "Nash, you already said all that stuff. Why don't you go to sleep?" From the back of the bus, Henry Harris added teasingly, "That's right, Mr. Nash. If you should die before you wake, maybe God will take your ass up to heaven or something." Uncle Nash answered, "God might take me to heaven, but can't no God send me to hell. I've already served my time in hell." I tried again to end this with a simple "Good night, y'all," but as was the case when Uncle Nash was truly worked up, Uncle William had the last word with, "Okay Nash, you are right. You know about as much as God. Now let's get some sleep."

The next day as we were preparing lunch, Mr. Stevenson said, "Ooooh Weee! Mr. Bill, I'm so glad you got Nash to quit running his mouth. Nash ain't got no shit for you. You sure pulled him up in time, and got him to stop running that foul mouth of his." Since Mr. Stevenson didn't get into verbal contests, I knew he was simply being descriptive. However, sensing easy prey, Uncle Nash pounced on him. Starting slowly and in a sarcastic voice, he said, "Now look who's talking. Nigger, you ain't had your hand on a woman since Mary Helen left your old, simple, feeble-minded ass. Last I heard, the best you could do was get some of that booty hole from that old faggot Michael, down in Johnstown. Stevenson, as pitiful as you are, you don't even belong in this conversation. If you want to talk so much, then tell us how good that "he-she" Michael has been to you with his booty and that old nasty mouth of his, since you want to talk about who has a foul mouth."

I felt bad for Mr. Stevenson because he just didn't have the skills to deal with Uncle Nash, or for that matter, anyone else. We all knew that Mr. Stevenson didn't have a woman, and we knew that, between his bad physical appearance and his lack of conversational skills, he wasn't going to get a woman. Now, surrounded by heterosexual men who took great pride in their skills related to interacting with women, Mr. Stevenson was being shredded about homosexual encounters.

We all sat silently for a few seconds. I was hoping he'd find an effective comeback. Finally, Mr. Stevenson said pitifully, "You a goddamn liar. I ain't never had a man's mouth on me in my life, and I ain't never had my mouth on a man no kind of a way. I ain't never done nothing like that, Nash." He should have stopped there, since Uncle Nash felt sorry for him and didn't respond. But Mr. Stevenson, trying to deflect attention from himself, added, "Now, Henry might have done some of that shit when he was in the Navy. But not me. If I can't get a woman any time I want a woman, then I don't want anything."

Henry was on Mr. Stevenson like white on rice, screaming, "Mother-fucker, what the hell you know about what I did in the Navy? The shit that faggot Michael been doing to you got you talking crazy!" Before he could go on, I asked Henry to lighten up on Mr. Stevenson. Still angry, Henry said, "Well tell him not to talk that old dumb shit about me."

Trying to keep stuff flying at the same time I was trying to shift atten-tion from Mr. Stevenson, Uncle Nash asked with faked sincerity, "Jack Lee, what you think of these old men talking this kind of shit in front of your son? I guess you're sorry that you brought him up here. We're sup-posed to be enjoying the Memorial Day weekend, fishing and everything, and these guys have gone to talking a whole lot of old shit." Knowing that he was putting me on, I answered, "No, Uncle Nash. He's got to learn some time, and it's better that he learn from you and the rest of the guys. I don't want him out in the street stealing a drink of whiskey, and hanging with the wrong kind of people."

Uncle William added, "You said something there, boy. If that young boy of old man Humphries had been up here fishing with us and his fa-ther, he wouldn't be in the reform school now." Then Henry had to get his bit in, firing at me. "Ah, bullshit. Jack Lee just sitting there being nice because he don't want Omari to know the shit that he did in life. He don't want us rippin' on his ass, so he ain't saying too much of anything." I didn't want to respond, but my silence would have been taken to be a sign of, at best, ineptness or, at worst, a sign of agreement. So I sought an exit strategy with, "I'll say something. First, it is clear that you all have gotten drunk in the middle of the day. Second, I'm going to leave you to yourselves, and let my personal minister, Stephen, pray for your lost souls. Let me have another drink. Then, after I finish eating lunch, I'm going to do something for you jokers that my Uncle Sydney said the devil would never do. I'm going to leave you alone. I'll see you guys after I take a nap. Omari, we are going to be leaving out after that, so be ready. When you finish eating, shut the trunk of my car, and put some more ice on the fish."

Seizing another opportunity to mess with me, Uncle Nash told me, "Leave that boy alone. You were young once. That boy fished all day with you yesterday and early this morning. Shucks, he might want to go see some girls later on tonight. There are plenty of old country girls up here. He might want to run with his old Uncle." I merely said a polite, "Okay, Uncle Nash," and proceeded to finish my lunch. Afterwards, I went into the bus to sleep, but was kept awake by the men laughing at Uncle Nash's continued trash talking.

As I lay on my bunk with the fan blowing semi-cool air on me, I started thinking about Omari listening to Uncle Nash's views on God. I didn't want to encourage Omari to have doubts about God, but I did want him to see another man who stood up for what he believed in, regardless of the consequences. For far too long, African American males had been denied opportunities to move out of their racially designated places, to define their own spaces, to speak in their authentic voices. I wanted my son to see African American men who spoke their minds, and who would speak out strongly even if it meant speaking against God. Just as young men needed to know their "alphabets," they needed to have the strength of conviction to be champions for their people; to become the "drum majors for justice" that Martin Luther King Jr. described.

What Uncle Nash had to say about Jesus was a sharp contrast between what my father thought about Jesus. I can still hear Daddy's deep voice earnestly leading the Sunday morning devotions with, "Oh the blood, Oh the blood, Oh the blood done signed my name; Oh the blood, Oh the blood, Oh the blood done signed my name. What can wash away my sins, nothing but the blood of Jesus; what can make me whole again, nothing but the blood of Jesus . . . oh precious is the flow that makes me white as snow."

Those present for Sunday morning devotional services would go on and on singing about the "blood" until, other than most of the children, most people present were worked into a frenzy about Jesus having spilled his blood to save our souls. I was glad when some of the old saints ended the singing by signaling that Jesus was moving them. The signs of Jesus' presence within people consisted of Deacon Talley crying uncontrollably, Sis Glover speaking in tongues "Ooohkookkabamesiiii, Ak babbba hundra," or Sis Houston closing her eyes, looking at the ceiling, and chanting, "Your precious blood, Jesus; your precious blood, Jesus; your precious blood, Jesus."

I never understood Daddy's, Mama's and all of their Mount Sinai friends' fascination with or belief in the power of Jesus' spilled blood on behalf of our souls. Over time, I had decided that the belief in Jesus gave some African Americans a decent set of values; but Omari's poem, "Uncle Nash," stirred my many conflicts about Jesus and African Americans' belief in the miraculous effects of Jesus' spilled blood.

Uncle Nash

Uncle Nash shed his hip boots
poured gin into his beer
rested his wrinkled feet
on the small hickory log
and told me about Jesus Christ.

Boy, there ain't no Jesus,
and if there is,
He damn sure ain't no black man.
His eyes reddened,
but he spoke calmly
in that wise man tone,
which was normally
only used for discipline.

Son, what kind of Jesus
could have let those white men
rape my grandmother
against an oak tree
until her blood,

ran down her legs.
How could there be a Jesus?
and if there really is,
then goddamn him,
cause only a white Jesus
could have let some shit
like that happen.

I remember being confused
but I never wrote Jesus off
like Uncle Nash. Jesus,
I still don't know what to
think about you, the Bible says
that you got wooly hair like
a sheep, I've felt my hair, and
my hair, is wooly like a sheep too,
but now a days we call that nappy.

If you do exist,
help, cause brother,
yo' people still have blood
running down their legs.

I reread the poem just a few days after the October 16, 1995, Million Man
March in Washington, D.C., and felt great distress by the fact that
African American blood was running freely before the March, and it was
still running *after* the March. I realized that I was just as angry as Uncle
Nash, but that my anger was not directed at Jesus. Rather, I was angry at
whites who tried so hard to be liberal but were inherently racist, and I
was angry with myself for believing in them, notwithstanding their fail-
ure to deliver in many situations. I had kept my faith in the positive possibilities of good white folks, even though on a daily basis I saw the most
flagrant racism coming from some of the most liberal whites. Was my

faith without evidence any different from Mama's and Daddy's faith in Jesus?

I had a deep sense of hopelessness as I wondered whether the African American youths' bleeding had to flow to some natural completion, just like the great plains of Africa had to burn themselves out before new life began. It was so depressing to acknowledge that not even the beauty of a million men gathered with a common purpose could become the beginning of the end of the bleeding. My mind kept teasing me with the possibility that Uncle Nash's view was correct, that unequivocally Jesus hadn't and wasn't going to save any of our souls before or after we died. And, I wondered if, unlike Uncle Nash, I was simply too afraid to dismiss Jesus.

I knew so many young, African American males who had grown up in father-absent homes, and without the benefit of other positive male role models, they were suffering from inadequate self-esteem, were lacking in confidence, and were unable to speak publicly or self-disclose privately. Given all that they faced in a racist society, I thought African American males needed to be as uninhibited as Uncle Nash was when he expressed his convictions about God. Uncle Nash was the ultimate, fearless, free spirited, "bad nigger" whom I thought we needed more of in the African American community. Because he also had a long streak of doing good in him, he was a role model with whom I wanted Omari to have the maximum exposure.

THE LION SLEEPS

It's William, Not Bill

We are sitting around the Red Bus.
The old men are telling stories about Mr. Bill
over a pot of tomatoes and cuke-a-mers.
They tell of how Mr. Bill used to
chase them women and race American cars.
They say he would talk shit until his mouth turned brown
and fish so hard that he would leave the Juniata herself half-naked.
Uncle Nash said he once saw Bill
lift a cast-iron stove
just to get his quarter that had rolled underneath.
And as they go on about Mr. Bill,
Uncle William just remembers and smiles.
But remembering too long brings him pain,
knowing the powerful man he once was
has eroded so quickly into what he sees
in the mirror each morning.
The only shit he talks now

is to his doctor about dysentery.
Where Bill has fished hard, William hardly fishes.
And now he sits back painfully,
directing the younger men in
where heavy equipment should be moved.
Uncle William lives with Ms. Francis now
and rides shotgun everywhere we go.
Although Bill was only feared
and Uncle William is respected
he feels like the old lion
who through past works
no longer has to roar,
still somewhere not so deep
inside him is the urge.

FOR ALMOST two decades, being in camp had meant freedom from all forms of psychological discomfort. Now, each time I came to camp, I was excited about spending time with Uncle William, but was troubled by the prospect that each trip might be his last. During the summer of 1993, I met Uncle William at the camp only once; he had, by then, a number of diagnosed and undiagnosed illnesses. His digestive disorder required major surgery and it was followed by a series of complications. During a hospital visit, Mama asked what he wanted, and Uncle William replied, "Hell, Grace, I don't need nothing other than to be six feet under."

I tried to hold onto Mr. Bill and Uncle William, but both kept slipping away. Wishing for some sort of rope to keep us connected, I remained frustrated by looking in all of the wrong places. Without deciding consciously to do so, I started doing some of the things that Mr. Bill or Uncle William did at camp. I didn't see this clearly until one evening when Uncle Nash, Henry Harris, Omari, my nephew Daniel, and I had come in from fishing. After we cleaned the fish, I got ready to cook outside. The bottle-gas stove in the Red Bus had failed, and it was one more thing that didn't get fixed in the absence of Mr. Bill. As I was preparing to cook on my new Coleman gas stove, I told the guys, "Omari, hand me the salt and pepper. Daniel, let me have that cornmeal, and while the fish are cooking, go in the bus, or check the trunk of my car, and get the hot sauce, ketchup, and paper plates. You all relax while I cook because in the morning I want you to cut the grass. We also have to get some wire to repair this screen."

No one said anything. Hearing the silence, and seeking to fill my nagging void, I asked, "How many fish do you plan to eat, Uncle Nash? How about you Omari—two or three sandwiches? Henry, I've got you covered too. You just make enough of that tomato, onion, and cucumber salad for all of us." As I sat there cooking, taking fish orders, and giving assignments, I became very conscious of the fact that everyone was sitting around me the way we all sat around Mr. Bill when he was cooking and telling us what to do. The discomfort associated with that realization caused me to exclaim, "Wow, do you guys see what I'm doing? Do you see where I'm sitting?" Uncle Nash answered slowly and seriously, "Yeah, we see you. Somebody's got to cook now that Bill ain't here." Still amazed by what others had already noticed, I said, "I can't believe what is happening to me. I'm even sitting in his chair. Daniel, find that glass of his, and let me pour myself a drink in Uncle William's glass."

As I held Uncle William's glass in my hand I felt ridiculous, yet had a strong need to continue the charade. I popped the lid off a can of beer, and poured the glass full, letting the thick, white suds run down the sides of the glass and across my hand, and drip to the ground. Imitating Uncle William, I drank the beer straight down and said, "Ah boy!" Omari's forced laughter suggested that I was right to feel ridiculous. But I proceeded, pouring about two shots of gin and then adding beer until the suds overflowed. I managed to drink only half of it in one swallow. Even though the beer-and-gin cocktail would temporarily dull my feelings of loneliness, I knew that I could sit in Mr. Bill's chair, cook the fish the way Mr. Bill did, drink Mr. Bill's favorite cocktail, and give orders like Mr. Bill, but nobody in their right mind would believe that I could replace

Mr. Bill. As I tried to deal with the fact that neither Mr. Bill nor Uncle William were present, my thoughts drifted to the time when Jack would no longer be in camp. Depression crept all over me. Wanting to shut down my thinking, I poured myself another slug of gin, and attempting to dismiss my sinking feelings, said, "Come on you guys. Let's eat and then play some pinochle."

When I called him in July of 1995, Uncle Nash told me that Uncle William "hadn't been doing too well," and that he would meet us Friday afternoon, after he stopped by to see Uncle William in the hospital. When we met in Mount Union, we were relieved by Uncle Nash's report that Uncle William might be going home in a few days.

That night, we had a fire blazing about ten yards from where we sat playing cards. I realized that Uncle William's old, faded brown jacket had been hanging outside under the shed for the past two years, and, each time we came back to camp, the jacket had taken on a larger and larger presence. Now it triggered an increasing sadness that I couldn't stand any more; it was too unpleasant a reminder of Uncle William's absence. It had to go. Concealing my true feelings, I mumbled something about the jacket being moldy, and Uncle William never being able to use it again. Since it was a bit damp, I poured kerosene on it before putting it on the fire. I watched as the flames shot up, and then slowly began to consume the jacket, hissing and sizzling as the damp cloth disappeared.

As the flames settled down and the jacket smoldered, I saw clearly that the time had come for me to cope with the impending complete loss of Uncle William. His old blue-and-white flannel shirt, hanging inside the bus since his last visit, hung in a way so that I could see impressions of his elbows. I had been using it, too, as a security object to facilitate my acceptance of the transition from vibrant Mr. Bill to fading Uncle William. Through a side window, I looked at that shirt and saw the muscular, hazel brown arms that worked in the steel mill, held beautiful women, maintained the bus, caught so many fish, and threw me over his head and caught me when I was a child. Without saying a word, I got the shirt and tossed it into the fire. It was so dry that most of it was gone in just a few minutes.

Nobody said anything as I used the flames to purify my spirit. Self absorbed, I didn't even notice when the card game ended, shifting my attention only briefly when Uncle Nash and some of the others got into a car and headed for the Elks. I stayed by the fire, sipping gin and occasionally raking through the coals as if I were trying to find something. Omari and his friend Dave sat under the light, just as engrossed in a game of chess. A little after midnight, a car pulled up to the bus, and I thought Uncle Nash had returned early. Instead, a stranger got out and inquired, "Any of ya'll kin to Nash?" Sensing trouble and wondering if Uncle Nash had wrecked, I responded, "I am. I'm his nephew from Pittsburgh." Then the stranger lowered his head and informed me, "Well, your people from Johnstown called over to Ms. Sally's house to say that your Uncle William had a pretty bad heart attack." After pausing and taking a long caring look at me, he added, "You must be the nephew they mentioned. I can see the resemblance in your face. Your folks in Johnstown said that Nash needs to leave right away for Johnstown because they don't expect Mr. Bill to make it through the night. I'm sorry to come over here and tell you this. Your family has my prayers. You drive safely going to Johnstown this late at night."

Dave and Omari continued in silence with their chess game, and I returned to my fire. I felt a little relieved when Uncle Nash got back to the camp about twenty minutes later, complaining about so few people being at the Elks. After I gave him the message about Uncle William and the need for him to leave for Johnstown right away, Uncle Nash paused and said, "I'll be damned! Son, I ain't going nowhere tonight. As good as he was looking when I left him on Friday, I don't want to look at him in the condition he is in now. I'm going into the bus and get some rest. You call them back, and tell them I'm going to get some rest before I return."

I knew better than to try to persuade Uncle Nash to leave. As he entered the bus, I got my car phone and called my older cousin Jean. We almost began to argue after I told her that Uncle Nash said he needed his rest, and she excitedly directed, "I don't care what rest he needs. Put Uncle Nash in a car and you bring him to Johnstown right now!" Wanting to honor her wishes, but knowing I really couldn't, I told her, "Jean, I'll do the best I can, but you know Uncle Nash." She pressed on with, "I know him and you know him, but you just get him here. The doctor doesn't know if his brother will live through the night."

I entered the bus and told Uncle Nash what Jean had said. Without hesitating and with that look of determination he got when he began to curse God, he said, "Hell, Bill might not live through the damn night, but there ain't a damn thing I can do about it. Like I told you, I'm getting some rest. You suit yourself. Go on to Johnstown now, if you want to, and tell Jean I'll see her when I get there. Now I'm getting my rest. If he dies, he dies. Ain't a damn thing I can do, not a goddamn thing." Seeing him undress and listening to the finality in his voice made me happy; I didn't want to go to Johnstown either.

Around eight-thirty in the morning, Uncle Nash and I awakened. To make sure that he could drive safely, I drove behind him when he went to get gas and a cup of coffee. I noticed that he got no sugar, although he usually added several packages to a small cup of coffee. After he got into his car and headed for Johnstown, I returned to the bus where Omari and Dave were still sleeping. Based on the ache sitting in the back of my head, I knew that the combination of little sleep, their big beer consumption last night, and the bright morning sun would prove almost lethal for them. Even so, because of what I needed to do, I awakened them shouting, "Let's go. We should be able to get some bass down in Lewistown this morning. I still need to catch that big one I promised to get for Uncle William."

As we waded down the river, I promised to catch one that would be the size of the huge bass called "Bubbah" in a television commercial. On a mission, I waded into faster moving water above my waist, and made a cast to the front and side of a submerged rock. When the crab drifted past the rock and I felt the first pull on my line, I quietly said, "Omari, I got Bubbah."

I knew I had hooked a very large fish, and I quietly maneuvered it until he was at Omari's knees. When the fish's large, greenish black dorsal fins came into view, we both knew that this was a very special fish. A few minutes later, after I guided the fish back to Omari and he lifted it out of the water, I said, "Omari, let's go. I've done what I came to do."

We returned to camp without saying a word. As we were cleaning the fish, I broke the silence with, "Omari, you know, some people back in Johnstown, including some of our relatives, will never understand us staying up here to fish this morning." Omari replied knowingly, "What else were we going to do?"

I thought about how naturally sure Uncle Nash was that Dave, Omari, and I were going to fish that morning. I knew that Uncle William would want us to fish that morning, and I knew that to be with Uncle William we needed to do so. I also knew that I needed to catch "Bubbah," and Omari seemed to understand, because he kept casting to where the smaller rock bass were biting, and never once cast to the deeper water where we both knew the bigger fish were located. "Bubbah" had to have been in the river for a very long time; surely, this fish would cheer up Uncle William.

I didn't want to go to Johnstown, but that Sunday morning I felt just as compelled as the spawning salmon swimming upstream. I found my way to Uncle William's room, and although visiting hours had passed, the nurses permitted me to see him. Because I knew it would bring back pleasant memories for Uncle William, I kept on my seven-year-old fishing hat which was decorated with fishing lures, a "Run Jesse run" button, one stating "Subvert the Dominant Paradigm," and another which read, "I thought I made a mistake once in life, but I was wrong." Uncle William said I was the only man he knew who mixed some "damn politics with fishing." He also teased me about doing "a damn fool thing like putting expensive fishing lures on a hat and never using them."

As I entered his room, Uncle William gave me a big smile, and asked, "Did you all do much good this morning? Nash told me he left you up there at the camp to fish this morning." As I was explaining how many fish I had caught during the weekend, along with the big bass that I had caught that morning, Uncle William interrupted teasingly, "I know you had your son with you. If you caught that many fish, I know damn well he did pretty good. He probably caught that big one you claim you caught." Going along with the tease, I said, "Yeah, he did," and before I could tell him what Omari caught, Uncle William asked, "Did you get the pipe to the bus's water line fixed?" Hearing the question, I thought to myself, "Wow, Uncle William is recovering from a severe heart attack last night, and this afternoon he is concerned with whether we fixed the water line to the bus."

Not having the tools, the expertise, or the willingness to take the time to properly fix the pipe, I had "fixed" it by simply attaching a new garden hose to the main outlet. When I told Uncle William about the garden hose, he gave me a very puzzling look. It was almost as if he was saying, "Say it ain't so, Jack. Not you. You didn't do something as trifling as run a garden hose over to the bus, instead of using a little solder to fix the joint in the copper pipe?"

Before I could answer, Uncle William sat halfway up in bed and began to gasp for air. His eyes bulged to the point where I thought they would explode. He stared at me in a strange way that made me feel as though he didn't see me, and then his glassy eyes seemed to ask me a big, unanswerable "why?" I heard two more long, dry gasps for air, and then Uncle William fell back on his pillow, mouth open and eyes protruding. Somehow, I managed to unfasten my feet from the floor, and I ran for a nurse.

When I returned to his bedside, Uncle William was so still that I don't know why the nurses and doctors bothered with their frantic activities. They pounded on his chest, they injected him with something, and then they put me out of the room. Through the adjacent wall, I heard them plead, "Come on Mr. Young! Breathe! Breathe, Mr. Young!" I knew for certain, however, that after inquiring about the water pipe, Uncle William had decided to breathe no more.

Everyone Must Dance

I ripped the barbed hook out
of his bloody white mouth
tearing his amphibious flesh.

I flipped the rock bass onto
the grassy bank behind me
then turned to watch his dance.

He danced a brief lambada
and laid still in the grass
gasping for the unfiltered air.

As the sun penetrated our bald heads
I watched his scales toughen
as death began to claim him.

I watched as his eyes dried
while looking at Juniata's water
his school, his home, his mother.

I watched him die just as
God watches each of us die
waiting for each man to do his dance

Mine a medley; a grad school house
dance, followed by a freestyle career
dance, and a slow dance with Cherice
in our woods, no music, for a finale.

I watched the fish finish his dance,
hoping God will let me finish mine,
then carefully filleted him.

I gave his entrails to the river
left his carcass for the land animals
and took the meat to give me
strength to finish my dance.

I sat engrossed in fleeting thoughts, Uncle William's life passing before my eyes. The nurse dutifully said something about being able to pay my last respects after they cleaned Uncle William a bit, and the doctor came to me, offering an explanation of what all she had tried to do to save him. Given the consequences of two severe heart attacks in such a short period of time though, she said his death was "for the best." I heard what they were saying to me, but my mind was consumed by something else, something quite otherworldly.

Uncle William died talking with someone he loved about something they both loved. I felt simultaneously good and guilty for feeling good. Then I flashed back to the approximate time of Uncle William's first heart attack and the fact that it occurred at the same time I was burning his jacket and shirt. The possibility of something more than a coincidence was too much to ponder, and I quickly dismissed the thought.

I drifted through the next two days of telephone calls. During the funeral, at the request of the family, I delivered remarks. I chose to talk about "a mighty good man." As I spoke, it was as close as I had ever come to feeling nothing. Two days after Uncle William's funeral, I received a poem from Omari; as soon as I saw the title, "The First of the Great Ones," a sunny sensibility replaced the lingering gray cloud that had engulfed me since Uncle William's death. The poem also shifted my perspective regarding the finality of his death. Uncle William and Mr. Bill were gone, but I took comfort in knowing that the great ones would continue. "The First" gave me hope that a new generation of great ones would come forth, and it reminded me of the great ones still in my midst. Of even greater importance for me, however, was the fact that the poem helped me to clearly see and accept a redefined relationship with Omari.

This poem was but one of several that revealed themselves as threads in a binding rope extending from him to me. That I was on the other end of Omari's rope, and that his poems had been woven from the substance of our experiences, were truly transforming realizations. As the poem's full impact settled in, I realized that Omari was now doing some building on the notion of the ark upon which I was so intent. While facing a low point in my life, his poem helped take me safely across an emotional abyss. I never again wondered whether Omari could write; instead, I wanted to write with him in order to tell others about how important relationships were built, and how they served as the vehicles for getting through turbulent waters.

The First of the Great Ones

Uncle William was the first
of the great ones to go.
News of his heart attack was
relayed to his brother Nash,
my father; and me on the river.
"Doctor said he wouldn't make it
through the night" but we
didn't cry or leave
we knew to play cards and
to drink gin for him
and in the morning
we knew to keep fishing.

After cleaning our catch,
I packed and headed back
to Maryland where the answering
machine was already blinking.
My mother's voice claimed
that Uncle William was gone,
it seems that he had lived

through the night,
he had waited for Nash
and my father to return.

He wanted to know
how the fishing was
my father told him.
He wanted to know
how the camp was
my father told him.
He wanted
to know who had caught
the biggest bass and
as my father was telling him
the story, William grinned
and waited patiently
for him to finish
before bugging his eyes
and dying calmly
Saturday July 8th 1995

12

THE LEGEND

Gnats

Each year as May dances her finale
there is a brief intermission
on the Juniata River so
the gnats can clean the stage
before June's annual due with the sun.
The gnats form black tornadoes
and settle discrepantly
on the grass, the water,
on deer shit, on us,
each fisherman must battle
the hungry swarms with the
tools that age and wisdom
have equipped them with.

The tornadoes touch down
on my younger cousins,
the gnats hone in on their
younger bodies' oils and fragrance

quietly biting all exposed skin.
As soon as they leave the camp
the gnats set upon them,
forcing my cousins into guerilla warfare
running, hiding, and swinging blindly
at their relentless oppressors.
At the end of each day,
tradition mandates we show
their swollen bodies no sympathy,
we ignore them, and share no remedies,
we remember what it was like
to reek of youth and inexperience,
to have that sweet smell of puberty,
to have so many lessons to learn,
and to feel the wrath of the gnats.

When the gnats come for me,
I use science to disguise my youth.
Two parts Off and three parts Muskol
applied heavily to my skin and hat
hide my inexperience from the gnats,
but as soon as my potion wears off,
the gnats dive into my eyes,
scorning me for my treachery.
The old men don't help me
and so as my eyes redden
and fill with the tiny black bodies
I suffer alone.

My father and uncles ignore the swarms
they don't flinch as the gnats
land on their faces and crawl
in and out of pores and across
the rims of their glasses.
I see how the gnats take their toll on them,
with their nonviolent disobedience,

my uncles and father are sent to bed
well before the rest of us
they sleep snoring like bears,
but always in fetal positions.

The gnats never bother William or Nash
Having fought their battles
they walk right through tornadoes
unharmed and the gnats un-offended.
One morning Uncle Nash
went outside with the scent of a young girl
he was with at the Elks the night before.
The gnats attacked him and he spoke
"Git from round me ya
muthafuckas, for I piss
on ya!"

The gnats were confused by the wisdom
and experience in the voice, but the scent
urged them on. My cousins wanted to help
but I reminded them that if
they ever saw Nash fighting gnats
and wanted to help,
"they were supposed to help the gnats!"
They held their ground and watched on.
Uncle Nash stood still, poised, accepting the bites,
as if he was absorbing strength from them.
He slowly took out one of his homemade cigars
and puffed out its thick gray smoke,
that had banned him from the houses of countless women,
the gnats got drunk on his toxins
and fell staggering about the earth
my cousins and I ran out to see who
could trample the most black bodies,
as Uncle Nash smiled down at us.

"OLD BUSTA LOOSE," as he called himself, satisfied the rebel side of me. I loved the way he would knock on your front door, and before you could answer, would yell, "You'd better hurry up and open this damn door before I knock it down!" He would walk into the crowded Coke Plant Club, raise his voice above the loud music, and yell, "I feel like busting loose tonight!" Men and women turned momentarily from their shot glasses, beers, and conversations. Some woman would invariably yell, "Look who's here!" With that, everyone focused on Old Busta Loose as he stood in the center of the floor, gyrating to the music, popping his fingers, and singing, "I feel like busting loose." Before the night was over, Uncle Nash's old body would have done the newest fast dance with all of the youngest women in the joint. In nightclubs and elsewhere, inhibition never took up residence within Uncle Nash, and I admired him for being one of the most free of all free spirits.

When I was a child, I didn't believe anyone could drive a car faster than Uncle Nash. He often packed me, my two older brothers, and one or two of my young cousins in his car, and took us for a ride that ended at Alwines Dairy where he bought us ice cream cones. As he approached another car, he would ask, "Do y'all want me to blister his ass?" We urged him with, "Get him, Uncle Nash! Get him!" The motor roared and the car lurched forward as he pressed the gas pedal to the floor, the acceleration causing the back end of the car to squat down. As Uncle Nash flew down the passing lane, we chanted, "Blister him, blister him, blister him, blister him." After he had passed the car, he would smile, and say, "If y'all want me to blister another one, I'll get him for you." We of course begged him to blister every car in sight, and he always did. When Uncle Nash blistered a car, I shared in what I believed to be his invincibility. In addition to enjoying this bit of life in the fast lane, I also shared vicariously in his romantic adventures.

Uncle Nash had very positive relationships with more pretty women in more towns than any other man I knew. From what I could tell, he never "loved them and left them." He just always loved more than one at any given time. Although I knew Daddy considered Uncle Nash's conduct with women to be a form of "foolishness," and Mama always said that it was "a shame the way that brother of mine carries on," I admired his relationships with so many different women. He seemed to be as much a man of integrity with two or three women as Daddy was with one woman. To me, he was at his romantic best when he returned to his home in Virginia.

Each time that Uncle Nash drove me and my two older brothers to Virginia to spend the summer, he would make a stop at an old jook joint located about an hour's drive from Uncle Youngie's and Aunt Minnie's house. Jones Paradise was the "in" place for fast-lane colored country boys throughout Goochland County. Inside Jones, as they called it, one could savor aspects of the southern good life: home cured ham and fried chicken sandwiches, thick butter bean soup, hamhock-laced collared greens, chunks of deep yellow cornbread, thick brown biscuits, and the very best moonshine to be found outside of Georgia. There were also women such as Peaches, Little Bit, and Bertha Mae who were well experienced in the dancing they called "belly rubbing" and "grinding." While Uncle Nash was inside Jones Paradise, my brothers and I sat in the car and devoured the fried chicken sandwiches and cold bottles of Royal Crown cola that he brought us.

One night when Uncle Nash opened the door to Jones Paradise, a gorgeous woman—what we called back then a "light skinned, red-boned, big breasted woman"—Phoebe Boatwright, screamed, "Lord have mercy! My man done come back home! Come on in here, daddy, and let mama give you a little sugar!" Uncle Nash quickly threw one arm around Phoebe Boatwright's shoulder. As they turned their backs to us, and just before they shut the door, I could see that the woman had a butt made of two hams just like the two Mabel had in grade school, only this woman's hams were much bigger and shook as she walked. Uncle Nash must have gotten a lot of sugar that night because ordinarily he would have returned in an hour or so. Waiting for him, the pace of my heart quickened just by wondering what it would be like to get a little sugar from Phoebe Boatwright.

Until he returned to the car, we usually argued about things such as whether Uncle Nash stopped to see the same woman, and why so many women loved him so much that, as they said, they "loved him to death." The most vociferous arguments occurred when we tried to determine which one of us would grow up to be the most like him. Usually, we were still talking when Uncle Nash got back, but the night Phoebe Boatwright met Uncle Nash at the door, we fell asleep waiting. The sun was coming up when he opened the car door and laid a quart-sized mason jar of moonshine on the back floor of the car. After giving Phoebe Boatwright a big hug, he said romantically, "I'll see you on my way back to Johnstown." Then she fluttered her eyelids and gave him a kiss on his cheek, leaving traces of her pink lipstick. Looking into the car, she asked, "Are those Grace's children who done grown like weeds?" Uncle Nash laughed and replied, "Every one of them is Grace's." Then, after scanning me from head to toe, she exclaimed, "Great day! Look at the long legs on that little Jackie Lee! Boy, step out of the car so I can see you."

As soon as my feet hit the ground, two huge soft arms engulfed me. She lifted me off my feet to give me a hug, and my face sank into the deep crevice of her warm, oversized breasts. Momentarily, I lost my breath and couldn't see anything, but felt what seemed to be two huge warm water balloons. I enjoyed the smell of her skin, which had been dusted with a white powder, producing an aroma similar to the vanilla flavoring Mama always used in her sweet potato pies. As the multiple pleasant sensations rushed through me, she released me, saying, "Get your little sweet self on back in that car." That experience of being hugged by Phoebe Boatwright was like going down the big dip of a roller coaster, and the thrill was over before I knew what had happened. While I was sitting in the backseat, still caught up in that wonderful moment, Uncle Nash looked over his shoulder, gave me a smile, and winked. When I winked back, he laughed heartily, started the car, and as he pulled off, said, "Girl, I'll see you. You're a mess."

Almost every day of his adult life, everywhere he went, Uncle Nash wore a suit. He went to work in the steel mill, he wore a suit; going to and from fishing, he had on a suit. Some days, he fished in a suit, and he always wore a suit underneath his hunting clothing. After he retired, Uncle William tried to get Uncle Nash to purchase a few flannel shirts and khaki pants to relax in, at least for hunting and fishing, but he was relaxed when he had on his suits. When he had on one of his best suits, sat with his legs crossed, held a cigar in one hand and a drink in the other, beautiful women found him irresistible. Even other men admired him.

Watching Daddy, I learned how a man should dress for church and special events. Watching Uncle Nash, I learned how to dress for success in the social world, particularly when a woman's love was what a man sought. Daddy taught me how one could love one and only one woman, but Uncle Nash taught me how one could love and appreciate many women. Although I chose to follow in Daddy's footsteps in this respect, other than my early childhood friends, my son and my youngest brother, most of my close friends have been women. Given the way I idolized the well-over-six-feet, honey-colored, wavy-haired, cigar-smoking, fancy suit-wearing, great hunter, fisherman, and Romeo who was my Uncle Nash, it was quite a moment for me when he asked my son to start bringing a suit with him to our fishing camp.

For years, Uncle Nash slept in the bus only some of the time. After fishing all day, he often left our camp at night and headed for the Elks, dressed in his suit, tie, and a wide-brimmed straw hat with a red paisley band. For him, the Mount Union Elks was second only to the Johnstown Coke Plant Club. Occasionally, Uncle William and Henry Harris went with him to the Elks, but, for the most part, Uncle Nash went on his own. On Omari's first fishing trip after high school graduation, Uncle Nash told him, "Boy, don't you come up to the camp anymore without a suit and tie. You're old enough to travel with your Uncle Nash now. Your Daddy is married, but you ain't. From now on, after we finish fishing, you're going with me over to the Elks. There are enough women over there for me and you too." I thought this invitation was one of the best graduation gifts Omari received. Very few received an invitation to "run" with Uncle Nash; certainly, I never did. This special recognition he had given reminded me that many days had passed since Omari rode on my shoulders, tied to the rope, while I waded the river.

Uncle Nash was a better hunter than a fisherman. Some even complained that he took the fun out of hunting by being so quick to throw the shotgun on his shoulder, aim, and drop a rabbit with one shot. He could have been a great fisherman, but once he went over to Mount Union at night, he often stayed there until nearly noon the next day. On other occasions, he came back to camp around three or four in the morning, cursed as he undressed and used the piss bucket, and then stumbled into his bunk where he remained until late the next morning. By the time he recovered from the night before, Omari and I would have fished several hours and returned to camp. We always came back for him though, because fishing with Uncle Nash was a special treat.

Young and old people loved to fish with Uncle Nash because he talked more trash and created more excitement than anyone else. He never focused on catching the biggest or the most fish; rather, he was always creating excitement around whatever fish he or someone else was catching. His fishing was like his loving of a woman, since in the case of each, he seemed to focus more on the excitement of the catch than on the securing of a trophy. He always ended up with outstanding examples of each, though.

When it came to agitating in a quick-witted fashion, or what we called signifying, Uncle Nash was always right in the mix. The first time Omari's friend Dave came to camp, Uncle Nash introduced himself with a deceiving smile and said, "Hi, I'm their Uncle Nash Young. From the looks of your face and judging by your size, it looks like my Daddy might have had something to do with making you." Dave stood in a silent daze as Omari, Uncle Nash, Henry and I laughed, but soon he too relaxed into a smile when Uncle Nash told him, "I'm just playing with you son. This is just old Uncle Nash talking shit. You stick with these boys today, and you'll catch a lot of fish." Having again disarmed Dave, as he was walking away, Uncle Nash mumbled just loud enough for us to hear him, "Still, it looks like my Daddy has been in your family some where."

Uncle Nash was one of those people who others said "wasn't afraid of anything." I always believed he wasn't afraid of anything because he was the first person I heard say he wasn't afraid to die, and he meant what he said. Only those known in the African American community as "bad niggers" weren't afraid to die, and nobody messed with "bad niggers," unless they weren't afraid to die, either. I was also impressed by Uncle Nash not being afraid to die, because death really shook up most of my other relatives and their friends. Death caused a whole lot of screaming, crying, cursing, hysterics, arguments, and fainting. While death drove many of my family members crazy, death was also the only thing I knew that could cause one or two of my heavy drinking relatives to get sober for a few days.

Daddy, of course, never engaged in such family foolishness. When someone died, Daddy quietly helped to make the arrangements with the mortician and the minister. He also made sure that all aspects of the service were in proper religious order. Uncle Nash also remained calm, stating, "Hell, if you're dead, you're dead. All of us have to die some time. Ain't no sense in me getting all worked up."

Uncle Nash's fearlessness about dying got put to the test when he needed kidney surgery. I drove to Johnstown to visit him hours after his surgery. As I came around the corner of his hospital floor, I quickened my pace, realizing that I was a bit anxious about how he had come through the procedure. To my surprise, he was sitting in a chair, looking better than I had seen him look in the past year. His skin was almost as smooth as a baby's bottom, and his gray hair contrasted with it beautifully. Before I could comment, he told me, "Jack Lee, all of the boys around Johnstown couldn't believe that I wasn't scared. What the hell did I have to be afraid of anyway? I've lived a long time, and there ain't no point in living if you got to go through a lot of pain and all that shit. I was up in the old folks home the other day, and, man, I saw all of those old people just laying there, suffering, and stinking. I said to myself, hell no. I don't want to be like them. I told the doctor that if he opened me up, and saw that he couldn't do me any good, then just close me up and let me die right there on the operating table. That's the truth, and when I woke up this morning, I said, well, everything must have gone all right. If I get well, I would like to go fishing with you and that son of yours a few more times. You know how I have my fun up at the camp. When you think we'll be going? You just let me know what time you'll be going, and I will be ready. I'm going to fish with you all until I can't fish any more."

Sure enough, a group of us were seated around the metal-topped table during the first outing of the year. It was on this trip that Omari broached a painful reality. Slowly and seriously, he said, "Daddy, the camp is on its last legs. Look at the grass and weeds growing under this bench. I'm telling you, this camp isn't going to last that much longer."

Reluctantly, I agreed and added, "Yeah, and Uncle William would never have let this happen. The water isn't even connected. And look at how long our neon light flickered before it came on. When I checked, there was no bottle gas in the cooking stove, and no oil in the furnace." Then came Omari's pointed question.

"So why isn't anyone doing anything?"

"Because we all depended so much on Uncle William, and mostly, we just came up here to fish and have fun."

"That's not all. You guys are getting older, missing more days up here. I haven't seen Mr. Revere since the early part of last year. When you guys get up here, more and more you take midday naps when we usually would have been fishing. Even you don't get up as early on the second day."

Having listened to me and Omari, Uncle Nash added, "Hell! There's no damn point in talking about what ain't happening. Let's take some time and fix up this damn place. Right now, I'm going fishing." Not wanting to drop the subject, I said, "Okay, Uncle Nash, but a couple of us could at least pick up these cans and bottles before we leave. Omari and Henry, help me pick up this stuff."

After cleaning up the place a bit, we decided to go down to the falls where Uncle Nash could sit on the bank and catch a few nice fish. Omari went out on the ledge of the first rock over which the water was flowing, and I went about fifteen yards beyond him to another pool. Suddenly, we heard the familiar cry, "Water flashing!" Sitting in his favorite spot, Uncle Nash had a hold of what he had always called a "dooozie marooozie." A more than seventeen-inch bass soared into the air and made a big run for the deepest part of the pool we were fishing. Omari sat watching with a big smile on his face, and I began to watch this old, gray-haired man, with one kidney, fight a dooozie marooozie one more time. The bass made several more jumps and runs, and Uncle Nash had him at the bank with his head out of the water. The fish was wider than my hand. Unable to stand without slipping, Uncle Nash tried to use the fishing line to lift the bass out of the water and swing the fish over his shoulder. On the fourth attempt, the line snapped and the bass was gone.

Talking much stuff, Uncle Nash declared, "Shit! I wasn't going to keep that damn big fish anyway. They don't eat too good when they get that big. And you know bass aren't in season yet. Ain't no way I was going to keep that fish." I asked him if that was so, then why had he tried so hard to get the fish out of the water. Uncle Nash's silence, combined with the grin on his face, indicated that he truly was satisfied simply to be sitting in the sun after just having fought a dooozie marooozie. That was enough for him to let me have the last word.

We finished the day of fishing, made plans for the next trip, and departed. During my drive back home, a strange feeling came over me. I hadn't noticed anything coming to camp because I was so anxious to get there. Now, I was very aware of the fact that I was in one car headed for Johnstown, and Omari was in another headed to Maryland where he was attending graduate school. Driving back in the past, we would discuss all of the ones that got away, the ones that didn't, the ones that fought hard, what Henry Harris said to Uncle Nash, how Daniel fell into the water several times, and other minutiae of the trip. As I drove and talked, Omari and Daniel ate their sandwiches, fell asleep, and eventually woke up as soon as I was close to home. Now, I was alone with my thoughts.

I wondered how I would find enough time to fish and keep the camp in good condition, and I thought about Uncle Nash's health. Traveling through the mountains, I considered how amazing it was that Uncle Nash had driven himself up to the camp, had fished more than I thought he would be able to, and had remained in Mount Union to spend some time with his lady friend. All of this filled me with hope of another complete fishing season with him. When I got on the last seventeen-mile stretch, I called Omari on my cellular telephone. In a playful voice, and without saying "Hello," Omari answered, "Daddy, what do you want?" I started talking to my son, and enjoyed. as Mama always said, "hearing the sound of his voice." The next thing I knew, I was pulling into my driveway.

We fished with Uncle Nash the rest of that summer, and made plans for completely overhauling the camp the next spring, after Uncle Nash declared one evening as we were eating, "You boys are fuckin' up now. You said you were going to take care of this place, and now bushes are growing every damn place I look. You know Bill never would've let this shit happen, so y'all have got to do better. Have your fun, but take care of the place." Stepping in because I wanted to enjoy the rest of the trip and didn't want to hear more from Uncle Nash, I told him that I would take a week's vacation as soon as the weather broke in May, meet Henry Harris, Omari, Dave, and Daniel at the camp, and fix everything in need of repair. With that, he said, "All right now. Don't let me come up here in May and see this place in worse shape. If I do, I'm going to whip some of your young asses."

Before Uncle Nash had a chance to see us make good on my promise, however, he finally met up with death. Interestingly, he had said many times, "When I die, I want them to take me to the hospital and pronounce me dead on arrival. D.O.A. That's the way I want it to be. And I don't want all that crying and shit. Live your life while you're able to live it, and when you're dead, you're dead." He got his wish.

One night, Uncle Nash complained of a stomachache, collapsed on the floor, and when he got to the hospital, was pronounced dead on arrival. The funeral that followed was truly that of a fallen hero. The church was packed, standing room only. The service was as a celebration, just as Uncle Nash wished. I never heard as much laughter during a funeral service. At one point, my brother Stephen assumed his ministerial role and gently reminded us, "Folks, we are still in a church."

So many people wanted to offer personal testimonies that their remarks had to be halted after about the fifteenth person. His nephews spoke about things such as "the first time Uncle Nash let me have a few drinks and got me drunk," "how Uncle Nash taught me to dress," "how happy I was when Uncle Nash bought me my first shotgun," "Uncle Nash was the one who taught me to how to show proper respect for a woman," and all agreed when one proclaimed, "Uncle Nash showed me how to be a real man." One of his nieces seemed to speak for all of them when she testified, "There will never be another man like my Uncle Nash!"

All of his peers wanted to "say a word or two" because Uncle Nash was a totally free spirit who lived life more than to the fullest, doing things other men only thought about doing. Fear seemed to have no room in his person, neither of God nor man. This point was made well when Mr. Sims talked at length about the time that "Nash refused to back down from the white boss in the steel mill, even though it could have cost him his job." Not one of us had another example of someone who had lived life harder, enjoyed life more, and made life so much better for everyone he encountered. That day, we celebrated a man who had busted loose on life. Those who truly knew him understood why the extended family enjoyed Omari's poem, "Uncle Nash AKA Old Busta Loose."

Uncle Nash AKA Old Busta Loose
(Too Funky for the Devil and Too Good for God)

Anybody here whispering
it was just his time,
                    or
it was just old age,
                    or
the lord just called him home,

ought to be slapped in dey
muthafuckin mouth
                    cause
anyone who really knew
Nash Young knows
Dat's all bulllll . . . shit!

Why da hell y'all wanna
talk all dat foolishness
                    when
you know old Busta Loose
                    just
had to bust loose one more time?

He had to bust loose from a body
that wasn't worth a shit
A body that had the nerve to be
walkin slow, and needin medication,
                    a body
shakin when he tryin to play cards
or sip a beer to knock the chill off,
                    a body
that had the audacity not to be able
to see straight enough to shoot
the left nut off a squirrel

or
have sense enough to rise
around a pretty young girl

He had to bust loose from a body
                    that
some of y'all mighta sworn
was headed straight ta hell
                    but
anybody down to the Coke
Plant Club could tell ya Nash
was too Funky for the devil
                He'd
probably take one look down there,
wipe his sweat, piss on the floor,
and ask the Devil how da hell
he was supposed to bust loose
with all these hot ass lights on?
                Devil
would just slap him five, light
his cigar with his best flame and
ask him where he got dat bad ass suit.

He also had to bust loose from a body
some of y'all swear is going to heaven
                    all
of us at the fishing camp been waitin
for this to happen for years, though
                probably
        for all the wrong reasons . . .

            we know
He will kick in the pearly gates
                unless
there are two female angels at the door

then
of course Nash will gently knock twice
but
after that he's coming for you God
and
you know you owe that man some answers
So
Lord I have some advice for you:

Just answer his questions as best you know how
and don't beat around the bush,
Oh,
and make sure you put a cloud or two in front of your face,
cause if you don't, and it turns out
you really a white man after all,
I'll see plenty of black rain, or blue lightning,
and
I'll know Uncle Nash done Busted Loose again
and
the apocalypse will soon be here!

WE FISH

We Fish

My grandfather stays with my father
because he fishes.
Wading these motherly banks
of the Juniata evokes memory.
Each cast, each fish,
keeps the memory of his father fresh.
This is how we beat death.

I know if Alzheimer's ever claims my
father, as it did his, all I have to do
is fish. I will fish the Juniata, and
let the memories of my father flow
through me. Fishing for channel cats,
doing the Juniata float, and sneaking
down the back side of the church
to fish on Sundays. I will fish
because we fish, and they fished, and
I know my father can never leave me,
if I just fish.

WHEN MY father retired, although it was his life and not mine, I tried to figure out what he would do with the rest of it. After two discussions, I gave up because he would only say, "We'll see, we'll see." Years later, at the time of Daddy's death, my son's poem caused me to wonder what implications my interactions with my father and my son might have for young African American males on the road to manhood.

As Omari's poetry continued to unfold, I realized that I didn't know a lot of things I desperately wanted to know. I didn't know if Omari recognized the potential insight and power behind beating death and living beyond death, or if he was using writing to facilitate his own mourning. I didn't know why Omari's young mind was contemplating concerns of old souls, or especially why I was wary about his ability to write, when the things he wrote so consistently pulled on my mind like an ocean's undercurrent. And what was he doing helping me to address life's major issues, as opposed to me helping him? After all, I was the father. Sure, I had tried to help my father deal with important issues in his life, but that seemed different because his were the too-familiar problems associated with aging. It was scary to think that I might already need some help from Omari — that he was helping me at a younger age than my father needed me to help him. Could it be, for reasons unclear to me, and which I might not wish to acknowledge, that I, too, needed the help of a son?

Daddy was a hardworking man for whom "foolishness" consisted of just about everything but work, and anything less than hard work wasn't really work. When you saw him, he was wearing either work clothing permeated with dirt and sweat or he had on one of his finest wrinkle-free dark suits because he was attending to either church or Masonic business. During my entire life, I never saw Daddy wear a pair of shorts, a sport shirt, or flamboyant shoes, all of which he associated with foolishness. Although he had hunted and fished to supplement his family's food supply when he lived down home, and didn't view these activities as foolishness, he didn't have time for them in Johnstown. He did involve himself in our fishing mania, but in his own way.

Before the days of our fishing camp, all of my equipment was stored in my parents' home in Johnstown. After I moved to Pittsburgh, part of a fishing trip would include stopping in Johnstown to get my gear the night before, and stopping again on our return trip to clean the fish. These stops allowed Daddy to get involved in some of what he considered to be the more "serious" aspects of our fishing, and provided the opportunity for us to be workmanlike together.

Part of the Johnstown routine was that Daddy always asked, "What time are you planning to leave in the morning, Jack Lee?" although everyone knew we would be leaving sometime between four-thirty and five. I always set my alarm clock for four, and, for years, was the first to rise. Hearing me, Daddy came downstairs and helped load the car. Eventually though, he began to wake up first, and those going fishing awakened to the smell of the thick slabs of bacon and specially seasoned hot sausage he was frying. He would have put some of Mama's fresh rolls in the oven, and then started cooking eggs once we were all assembled in the kitchen. When Daddy first began the breakfast ritual, you could hear him cooking around three-thirty. As time went on though, he began cooking earlier and earlier, until one morning around two, I asked, "Daddy, what time is it?"

With a big grin, he answered, "I don't know son, but I know you all will leave here with your bellies full."

I headed for the shower because there was just no direct way for me to tell Daddy that he was getting up just a little too early; he loved the fact that we ate everything he cooked those mornings. He would never come with us, though. When we pulled off in the dark, he was usually standing in the basement doorway. After we circled the block and turned onto the main highway, he watched us until we passed the field adjacent to our house. I often wondered if he went back to bed proud of his morning's work, or if he ever, just once, wished he had left with us.

When we returned, Daddy had pots, pans, water, knives and scalers (kitchen forks) waiting for us in the backyard. Dressed in his old railroad work clothing, including his striped cap, he met us at the car with a smile. He continued smiling and talking throughout the hour or so of cleaning fish, inquiring as to who caught what, and musing on which he planned to eat.

For nearly ten years, Daddy's involvement with our fishing was limited to these activities. In the basement, he would line our boots up beside the rods, oil our reels, untangle our stringers, and hang them from nails in the rafters. When they had too much dried fish blood and dirt on them, Daddy washed our fishing vests and jackets. It was obvious that he enjoyed these chores, but it bothered me. At sixty-five, he hadn't learned how to enjoy himself in any non-work way. Why did he still always have to be so serious, tough, strong, and hard at work?

Upon returning one time, we found Daddy had gone so far as to build us a "bait box." He dug a hole about two feet deep, four feet long, and four feet wide. Then he added a three-inch thick base and four walls of concrete. The bait box was filled with alternating layers of dirt, shredded paper, and grass, and had a plywood top covered with tin. From then on, Daddy took great pride in going out the after dinner on the nights before going fishing and getting the thick nightcrawlers out of the box; between trips, he monitored its temperature and moisture, and on rainy nights, he picked up nightcrawlers to replenish our supply, claiming that his hardy breed helped us catch our largest fish.

Years earlier, Daddy had worked the daylight shift on the railroad. He would get home around four in the evening, eat dinner, and by five o'clock say, "Let's go." "Let's go" meant that my two older brothers, Russell Jr. and Sterlin, and I would be headed down to the foundation to work with Daddy building our house. During the summer, "Let's go" meant working until we couldn't see at night. When we got electricity, we worked until ten at night on Saturdays, and we probably would have worked longer if not for the fact that we attended church every Sunday. We did all of the work on our house except the electric wiring, the plumbing, and the laying of the cinder block foundation. Eventually, we had a four-bedroom house. During the years that we built our house, hearing Daddy snore was one of the most pleasant sounds in the world.

Daddy never once tossed me a baseball or football, but was always quick to say, "Jack Lee, I have a job for you to do," and quicker to manufacture one for me if he saw me engaged in the foolishness of playing a game of tag with my friends. He was always working with me, teaching me; he was so morally straight that, privately, I called him the Boy Scout. Throughout my childhood, I longed for him to do something with me other than take me to church to "learn lessons," send me down home to work on the farm in order to "do me some good," make me do jobs around the house in order for me to learn how to do a "good job," and whip me with his thick leather belt to teach me some more "lessons I would never forget in life."

During his first year of retirement, I encouraged him to go fishing with us. "Daddy, you should think about going with us. I know you would really love it up there. Old man George Brown is going on eighty-something, and he still fishes. You would like him." He softened a little. "Well, I'll think about it. Now that I'm retired, I ain't got much to do around here."

But Daddy never fished during that entire first year. His excuses ranged from needing to be around the house to "look after your Mama" to some church or Masonic "important business" he had to take care of that day.

A year later, he finally agreed to come along, but he refused to fish. I explained that I had brought enough equipment for him to use, but I quit trying to convince him when he stared at me and Daddy's eyes said, "I'll just watch you all."

At the first stop, Daddy stood on the bank and watched us wade the river. At the next, he followed us through the woods to one of our favorite spots. All day, each time that we came out of the water with fish, he smiled and said, "Well, if this ain't something."

That summer, he came with us on a second trip and continued only to watch, but at the second stop, while standing on the bank with a smile wrapped from ear to ear, he was joined by another senior citizen. I heard Daddy say, "Those are my boys out there catching all of those fish. That oldest one has his doctoral degree. That's my daughter-in-law who is doing pretty good too. She has a doctoral degree too."

All the way home, he talked about how glad he was to have "gone fishing." "Boy, am I glad I came along today. All of the time that I have spent in Johnstown, and this is just my second time to have gone fishing. Some places you all went today reminded me of fishing down home in the James River. The next time, I'll show you how we caught fish. Yes sir, I'm surely glad I came. When do you plan to go again?" I immediately answered, "Next week!"

On the ride back, Jerri kept complaining about the fact that she was hungry, thirsty, and needed something cold to drink. I was making good time cruising at seventy miles per hour, and said we would be in Johnstown in about an hour. As we came over the top of a hill, Jerri shouted, "Oh look! There's a Dairy Queen down there on the right! I sure could use an ice cream cone."

Without looking into the backseat, I said, curtly, "Jerri, please!" My father intervened with a stern "Jack-stop-your-foolishness-and-stop-the-car!" Stunned, I stopped the car. Jerri got her ice cream cone, and we continued in silence while she ate. Belligerently, I nudged the speedometer up to seventy-five, but waited until Daddy went to sleep before pushing eighty.

Back home, as we were cleaning the fish, I said, "Daddy, you know, as a senior citizen, you don't have to buy a fishing license." He repeated his plan to go with us the next time and I thought the free license had sealed the deal. Next Friday evening, though, as we packed his gear, I realized that Daddy had not just been "watching" on those first two trips, but observing, determining what his own needs and preferences would be. He had cut a broom handle, tied a rope to the handle, and on the other end of the rope he attached a clip that he could snap onto his belt. After that, he would use his "walking stick" to get through the woods and wade in the river; he let it float on the water while he fished.

He had also developed his own style of dealing with falling into the water. He just sat down, and then stood straight up again, claiming that it was an old trick he had learned down home while wading across creeks. When he reached into a pocket for a new hook, I noticed that his old spring jacket had been converted to a fishing "vest" by the addition of a few hand-sewn pockets. Later that day, when we got to the spot where the huge maple tree hung over the river, and Daddy cast near the submerged logs where I always fished, I knew that he had observed well.

Apparently, Daddy, though, still had to learn about chubbies. In the very first pool of water that he cast, he caught a chubbie, and promptly put the fish on his stringer. Laughing, I said, "Daddy, don't save that little fish. We're going to catch a lot of bigger fish without so many fine bones."

About fifteen minutes later, realizing that my fishing day was passing, but not wanting him to feel that I was "sassin'," I gently advised, "Daddy, let's move to another spot. Nothing is biting here but these little chubbies." Resisting more as a fisherman with the fever than as my father, Daddy replied, "You all go right on where you want to go. I'm enjoying myself right here."

Respectfully, we stayed almost another hour, until Daddy no longer got bites.

His next trip was the first day of black bass season. I kept telling him that black bass had to be at least twelve inches long to keep, otherwise the game warden would give him a huge fine for each illegal fish he had on his stringer. As we waded close to the bank, I exaggerated the size of the fine for each illegal fish, and made sure that he saw me release the first small bass that I hooked. After we took him to a shallow riffle where we knew that he could catch one or two legal bass, Omari and I walked about a half mile upstream, waded over into some very deep water, and began to fish back downstream.

About an hour later, as we were wading downstream and came within twenty yards of my father, a game warden drifted up to us in a canoe. First, he asked to see our catch. Omari showed him his three black bass that were about fourteen or fifteen inches long, and I held up my two that were about the same size. After nodding his approval, the game warden then proceeded to Daddy. "How's your luck, old timer?"

Without hesitating, Daddy proudly pulled his stringer of six- to nine-inch bass from the river and asked the game warden in a boasting fashion, "How's your luck?"

As I started adding up the fine in my mind, the game warden simply laughed, and proceeded downstream. Mystified, I moved closer and asked, "Daddy, why did you say that to that man? Did you know who he was?"

"No. He came up to me with some foolishness about how was my luck, so I showed him all these fish, and asked him how was his luck."

"That was the game warden. He could have fined you."

"For what? You can't get angry with a man when you ask about his life and it turns out to be better than yours."

For the next three summers, Omari, Daddy, and I always tried, at the very least, to go fishing on the Saturdays before Mother's Day, Memorial Day, and especially Father's Day. I know that Omari got tired of me pointing out the significance of three generations fishing together on those particular weekends, but it meant so much to me, especially given the plague-like absence of fathers from the lives of so many African American children. Depending on how Daddy was feeling, we would sometimes get in a few other trips in July and August. Watching Daddy have fun was often more fun than fishing. Privately, I ached with the pleasure of finally having fun with, instead of working with, my father. I tried to pack a lifetime of the fun-filled experiences I wished for as a little boy into those summers of fishing with Daddy. I admired how quickly he went from "just watching" and being a serious father to being just one of the boys. He laughed, he relaxed, and he found peace. On the river, Daddy found the closest thing possible to a cure for old age.

His health faded gradually, though, and the Father's Day weekend trip became the only one we ever made for sure. Mama started worrying endlessly, insisting that he was too sick to go fishing. Eventually, certain things did interfere. First, he had a bout with glaucoma, then his sugar started getting out of control; periodically, his potassium level got too low, which usually meant a rush to the hospital and a day or two of intravenous feeding.

Daddy started sleepwalking, which was particularly dangerous since his night wandering took him past a flight of steps. Soon came memory problems. At first, we chalked these up to his old age, but then he began to forget friends' names. Next came his incontinence, a series of tense family gatherings, high-stress long-distance telephone calls, and many visits with various doctors. Late-night calls started coming from Mama. "Jack, you all need to come home as soon as possible. Your Daddy is just lying here, and can't get up." Two days later, she called and said, "Jack, your Daddy doesn't know what he is saying anymore. He said that if I didn't straighten up, he was going to 'fix me up' with the scissors." And the week after, "Jack, I hate to bother you this early in the morning, but your Daddy isn't doing any good at all. He's starting to get body sores from being in the bed so much. He was going on so bad the other day, I had to tie him down. It was so terrible, son."

Given Mama's tendency to exaggerate and Daddy's tendency to obfuscate, I never knew what to believe. So one snowy morning, after receiving a pleading call from Mama, I took off from work and drove to Johnstown. I found Daddy sitting in the living room, watching a television game show. I casually asked, "Daddy, how are you feeling?" Just as casually, he answered, "Fine, son. I never felt better in my life."

The three of us chatted, and after I joined them in a lunch of lima bean soup and crackers, I became convinced that he was fine, at least for that day. I said goodbye, and drove back home in a state of bewilderment. The possibility that Mama had exaggerated angered me, but all through the two-hour drive in the increasingly heavy, blowing snow, I kept asking myself, "But what if he was really sick? What if he had merely faked good health in order not to worry me?"

Other incidents occurred, and eventually a new doctor made the dreaded diagnosis, confirming Alzheimer's. With Daddy's steady deterioration, the family considered putting him into a home with medical care, but as Father's Day approached, I talked with Omari about getting in one more fishing trip with Daddy. When I telephoned her, Mama agreed surprisingly quickly, with the admonishment, "Just don't let him drown. Russell will probably be glad to go. Maybe it will do him some good. Maybe God will bless him, and let him have fun with you and that child of yours. God knows I've done all I can for him."

When we got to the renovated Red Bus, I went around to the side of the car to help him, but Daddy was already out. His formerly feeble body marched up the three steps of the old Red Bus, changed clothes, came outside, and began to put on his boots. Omari and I glanced at each another, shrugged, and got ready as quickly as possible. We fished for hours, having safely seated Daddy on a huge rock, about twenty yards upstream from me and twenty yards downstream from Omari. Each time that Daddy caught a fish, he started laughing, and said, "Well, if this ain't something." As the warm, sunny day floated by, I got engrossed, and at one point when I looked back at Daddy, I found myself more than 100 yards away. Concerned, I began to work my way back to him. When I reached him, he held up a stringer of about fifteen fish.

The trip went so well that we stayed two days. When we first arrived at camp, I had put all of Daddy's medicines on a shelf in the Red Bus, but we didn't remember any of these medications until we were packing to go home. During that trip, I found myself excited about something other than fishing. It was unbelievable; for two days, Daddy had behaved as though he had no medical problems of any kind. Incontinence disappeared, his physical strength reappeared, and his wit was resurrected.

Amazed, I asked him if he realized that he hadn't taken any of his medicines. His old, alert self responded, "Why would I take something I don't need? Down home, I worked all day in the fields and I didn't know what tired meant. How am I going to get tired up here catching these fish?"

But it was now clear to me that many of his difficulties came from being tired of a life of hard work, a life which contained so little time to just have fun. He had grown tired of being poor, constantly working very hard, doing whatever it took to provide for his family in ways that made his children feel that they were somehow better off than the really poor people. He had grown tired from always being the good deacon, the good mason, the good husband, and, indeed, the good Negro man who didn't drink and throw away his money. I knew this weary, seventy-year-old man had to be tired of diapers, doctors, pills, bills, ambulances, Metamucil, intravenous feedings, confusion, bouts with depression, being bathed by others, and family members asking one more time, "Are you okay?" My daddy was just too physically strong and mentally capable to have gone down so fast, so I knew that he had to have been very tired from living. I was deeply bothered by the fact that I didn't know when he had grown so tired. I did know that, if possible, we had to go fishing again. I had to help him now. I had to get him to a place where he could forget he was tired.

We went on two other fishing trips that summer, having seen how much good the first had done Daddy. Each time, he simply was not the same old man being urged to death's doorstep by multiple illnesses. It was eerie to observe how much he walked, waded, and fished when, by all other reports, he was overdue for hospitalization, especially since he wasn't home for more than two days before all of his symptoms reappeared. The disease made him forget so many parts of life, but fishing trips made him forget the disease.

One day, after more than an hour of fishing, I realized how long Daddy had been standing in the hot sun. It was one of those muggy, eighty-five-degree summer days, and I worried about the possibility of him dehydrating. He wanted to continue fishing, but relented when I told him that we were headed to an even better spot. A train was approaching when we got to the tracks, and, without thinking, Omari and I ran across the tracks, leaving Daddy on the other side. As the train was passing, instead of standing still, Daddy started walking in the direction from which the train was coming. He was unable to hear us as we yelled for him to just stand still, that we would come and get him with the car. He kept walking, we followed, and when the train finally passed, we had to walk about 250 yards back toward the car. The sun was blazing, and Daddy was sweating profusely. I began to search my mind for the location of the closest hospital. As I was worrying, Daddy started laughing and talking.

"This reminds me of working on the railroad. That was hard work, all day long. We worked from when you couldn't see in the morning until you couldn't see at night. We called it the 'can't see to can't see' shift. Jack Lee, where's that better fishing spot?"

"Listen, Daddy," I said anxiously. "Let's get you in the car, and then I'll get us to the spot. Just stand here, and I'll drive the car back to pick you up."

He objected with, "No, son. The walk will do me some good."

And it did.

The day did finally come that Daddy had to be put into a nursing home. Omari and I stopped to see him each time that we returned from fishing. But soon he could no longer identify either of us. I engaged in painful, one-way conversations, as he just lay in his bed, curled in a fetal position, with his eyes closed. He lost so much weight so fast that you could almost see parts of him disappear. A 250-pound, muscular man had shrunk to less than 120 pounds. My father was residing in a body reminiscent of a young adolescent, but for his gray hair and wrinkled face. And his occasional grasp of my hand gave way to a rock hard, bony semi-fist tucked under his chin and pressed to his breast. For two years, he lay in this state. I kept talking to him, but my conversations got shorter and shorter.

In March of 1990, I received the final telephone call. After I hung up,

I thought about the trip when Daddy felt so well that he had forgotten to take his medicine, and how triumphantly he had said, "How am I going to get tired up here catching these fish?" I wondered how much longer he might have lived if we had been able to fish more often. I hated the fact that winter came early and cut short the fishing season, and my father's life. But, subconsciously, I hated myself for working so hard that I didn't take off to go fishing with him more often that last summer. I hated the fact that I was so much like him. I didn't know how much until he died. It scared me.

I got so much out of fishing with Daddy during those few precious summers that I was much better prepared for his death than I otherwise would have been. Ironically, with his passing, our fishing made me aware of a different sense of loss. When we fished, I sometimes felt as though I was taking my son, not my daddy fishing. I loved teaching my father to fish, but I wanted my daddy to tell me where to cast. I wanted my daddy to cause the formal walls of father and son to fall, and let us just be us by him slipping, falling in the water, then getting up and laughing because he too was fragile. I resented the fact that it took so long to get that close to my father and that it lasted then for such a short time.

I really wanted a father who, in addition to being a good provider, devoted family man, and strong disciplinarian, also took time to play catch football with you and took you out of school the first day of trout season. At the time of his death, I was still bitter that I didn't have this father as a child. Yet, I was even more grateful that Daddy had been so serious. Otherwise, I would have been unsuccessful in life, dropping out of school, drinking and committing crimes, like many of my friends with fathers who dwelled in foolishness. To cope, I decided to bury only the forgetful old body and not Daddy. I learned to live with both sides of him, the serious side that simultaneously disappointed and saved me and the fun side that temporarily revitalized him.

Reading Omari's poem triggered these memories and emotions about Daddy's strengths and frailties. It made me realize I need not always be so strong. Nor did I have to spend so much time trying to make my son hard and tough and serious. So, I became determined not to devote too much time to any one thing, causing me to miss opportunities to bond with Omari. I tried to be strong and serious as well as vulnerable and light-hearted, leaving Omari with more memories to appreciate than regrets. And so, we fish, keeping the memory of Daddy fresh, bonding with each other, perpetuating our family tradition.

14

AFTERWORD

WRITING THIS book with my son proved to be an overwhelming experience. At first, it was really uncanny trying to respond to Omari's many requests for me to edit my writing, especially when he challenged me to be "honest" with the "Jack character," as if I were some sort of abstraction that could be put on a shelf or studied in a laboratory. And I didn't initially understand what he meant; given how intense and personal the subject matter, how could I be anything but honest? Although it often seemed like he was badgering me, I pressed on, continuing to dredge up and filter many of my life's experiences through the prisms of his verse. The more I engaged in this personally challenging process, the clearer my relationship with the Juniata became, just like the muddy river itself gradually runs crystal clear as the debris settles following a summer thunderstorm. Some other very important things became equally clear.

For many years, my immersion into the Juniata and all that followed practically cured me of whatever ailed me mentally. The night after a long day of fishing found me, released from the "troubles of the world," sleeping peacefully, so much so that I had grown fond of referring to the Juniata as my "psychiatrist." But through revisiting these experiences with my son, I discovered an additional treatment for my psychological well-being. It was writing. No. It was writing *with Omari* about "Jack."

Writing about deeply felt matters and discussing them with Omari taught me more than I had ever wanted—but found I needed—to know about myself, as well as some very useful things about my relationship with my son. In addition to using A through Z to earn outstanding grades in school and a good job after college graduation, I came to understand how that alphabet could be used to work through stuff like Mama's incessant talking, Daddy's excruciating skinnings, Uncle Nash's God-cursing, and, most importantly, my uncontrollable fishing fever and the salvation that came from my fishing with my son, relatives and friends.

The writing process also held the promise, like fishing, of being another very good ark-building tool. Pushed to address feelings in a truthful fashion, I gained a deeper awareness of the fact that it doesn't matter if one is fishing or engaging in a host of other relational activities. The main point is to have nurturing relationships from which the involved vulnerable parties can grow. There is a need for various activities from which respect, love, personal pride, learning and sharing can come, and this was brought home to me by an African American female colleague. She listened to me discuss *We Fish*, and then said to me, "Sorry, brother Jack. I've got to tell you something right now because I don't want you to think that I stole your and your son's ideas. My Mama and I are working on a book entitled 'We Cook.' It's about how to deal with men, and many other early lessons necessary in life's negotiation. And when I was in the kitchen with my Mama on, uh, uh, uh, 'the apron string,' my mama shared all kinds of secrets with me. By the time that I was a teenager, I was cooking some things on my own. So just remember, I didn't steal your ideas, because we cooked before we fished."

Immediately, I saw that the ark-building materials for anyone are those that provide a locus for sharing personal information, passing on valuable traditions, and developing intimate bonds. By "holding onto apron strings," a young girl often has her sense of self-worth enhanced. For generations, when cooking together in kitchens, women have talked about their complex lives. Mamas have told daughters about how to deal with men, and they've taught many other early lessons necessary in life's negotiation. Indeed, whether the locus for interaction has been cooking, quilting, praying, shopping, or worshipping, many African American women have been much better able to move from "me," in the practice of individual personal activities, to "we," forming connections and solidarity in their relationships among themselves. Fortunately for me and my son, we had many opportunities to achieve similar results as we jogged, played cards, talked, fished, wrote, and grew. Unfortunately for so many young African American male youths, they have neither access to the support necessary for healthy interpersonal outcomes nor the appropriate opportunities for healing and self-renewal.

I continue to be deeply disturbed that too many African American males die having never had the opportunity of learning the meaning and importance of positive personal growth experiences. Their half-formed selves band together but most often not in the solidarity of shared, positive, meaningful experiences. Missing are the occasions for sharing and self-connecting. All too present are overexposures to extreme environmental hazards. Without healing opportunities, many young African American males engage in an array of counterproductive and self-destructive acts. In turn, they contribute disproportionately to prison building, one of America's turn-of-the-century growth industries.

The memories I have of fishing with my son, my father, my uncles, and my friends continues to give me hope in the midst of this despair. One experience I had while fishing with Omari particularly stands out for me as a metaphor for how we might approach the future.

When Omari was in fifth grade, a huge rock, along with other debris, slid down a hill and landed in the middle of a small creek, just where it had been trickling into the river. The rock was such an obstruction that,

following a rain, a mini-dam often formed behind it, making a temporary safe-haven for breeding mosquitoes and leaving stagnant water to
slowly dry up in the summer sun.

Over the years, the soil around the boulder began to erode, and
when it rained hard enough, a trickle of muddy water flowed around one
side of the rock and to the river. Eventually, there was enough rain and
erosion to let the water begin to flow around the other side. One day, I
noticed water flowing from beneath the rock. A few years later, following
a very hard rain, I saw water gushing over and around the rock. With the
passage of time, the rock was generally submerged. Today, the tiny creek
once again flows steadily into the Juniata, with the rock sitting in the
middle—not obstructing, but providing a nice holding place for fish. An
array of wild flowers and wild grasses now align the sides of the stream,
and, during the drier parts of the summer, I have seen deer come to drink
and graze. When I am in that area, I always cast over to that rock, hoping
to catch a fish, and remembering the obstacle that once was.

I am confident that African American men will, over time, transform
themselves and their circumstances. I have no doubt that they will remove the boulders in their lives. This faith in African American men
prompted me to write the following letter to Omari.

August 6, 2002

Dear Omari,
Last week's fishing trip was quite extraordinary! The upper-
nineties temperatures and low water conditions kept most fishermen
off the river, but we went to the County Line where we knew the
water would be deep. I was sweating profusely after climbing down
more than thirty feet of steep hillside to get to that part of the river.
Coming back up that hill, with a stringer of fish over my shoulder
and the sun still beating down on me, I thought about the drudgery

of football players at summer training camp. But the climb was worth it, given the remarkable number and size of the fish we caught.

When you waded in up to your neck, I'd never seen anyone wade across that part of the river. I thought you were just having fun by cooling off, but I learned otherwise when you began to hook and fight bass after bass. On the other side, standing in water above my waist, I caught my share. We must have set a record as we caught and released nearly seventy-five bass over the several hours that we fished. It was one of the most enjoyable spurts of fishing I've had since I began fishing the Juniata. And then an even better treat came when we went back to the cottage where Jerri had your son Javon.

You should see this picture that I took of you and Javon in the river. Javon has on nothing but his little red-and-blue rubber wading shoes, his bright yellow-and-red life jacket, and his soggy diaper. I have another picture of him holding that little four-foot "Ugly Stick" rod and reel you purchased for him, and wait until you see the shot of him holding the bass that you helped him catch: quite an achievement for a one-year-old! Seeing you with Javon in the river, I thought about the wonderful times you and I had spent on the Juniata, the joyful years that lie ahead for you and Javon, and my favorite places on the river that I want to take Javon. Then, my mind turned to the raising of another Daniel man.

Raising Javon is going to be tough because our society continues to be a perilous place for African American males, no matter what you, Cherice, and other parents do to protect them. Pediatricians will provide sufficient assistance regarding things such as Javon's shots, rashes, and treatments for the usual list of childhood diseases. Educators will offer a plethora of advice regarding literacy, social and emotional development, methods of discipline, and self-confidence. And you can count on your relatives for "tonics" and "treatments" related to things such as the use of cod liver oil to "clean him out," a drop of whiskey in two tablespoons of honey and a cup of orange juice to make him a "cough syrup," wiping his face with a pee-soaked diaper to "clear his complexion," and how to give him that "look" which will make him immediately stop the wrong thing he is doing.

Of course, you and Cherice will test your own hypotheses regarding the raising of this Daniel man. However, much like his father and his father's father, Javon has a mind of his own and he will never fit neatly into any round, square, or other geometrically-shaped holes that are said to be signs of "normal child development." Last week, you saw how he insisted on holding his rod by himself, even though he could not wind the reel. And twice he proved his willingness to jump off the dock into the river. As Javon continues to march to the beat of his drummer, and as you witness African American males continue to be victims of the many societal pitfalls, you will have many reasons to worry about his healthy growth and development.

Notwithstanding all that you and Cherice do for and with him, you will wonder if he will reach manhood, unblemished by racism, unencumbered by the weight of adverse economic circumstances, and unequivocally qualified to pursue a life of self-actualization. You will pause longer when you hear a news story regarding an innocent, academically talented, African American male college student being shot and killed by police officers who claimed that they thought his umbrella was a gun. You will flinch harder when you hear about the African American male high school valedictorian who was stopped by the police on the night of his prom, for no other reason except that he was driving a late-model car like the one that you will permit Javon to drive. You will appreciate better the fervent prayer, "May my child outlive me," the next time that you read about African American children caught in the crossfire of a drive-by shooting. Concern for the well-being of Javon will dwell within you beyond the days that your "nest" should be empty.

It took me a very long time to see that you were going to be okay, a realization that came quite unexpectedly when you helped me to understand myself and my concerns for the healthy survival of African American males. A huge burden was lifted from me when I came to fully appreciate some of your poems, especially the ones related to our fishing expeditions. While I was still worried about your well-being, you helped me appreciate how fishing provided me with an anti-stress medicine more effective than any pill, and how it contributed significantly to the positive bonding between me, you, and all those other guys who fished with us. You were okay, in part, because our fishing had provided us with a stage upon which several generations of African American males had played significant, life-enhancing roles. Grandfathers, great-uncles, fathers, sons, brothers, and other old men, not related in any way at all, had leading parts.

Growing up under the watchful eyes of my parents and our extended church family, I'd heard so many references to "and a child shall lead you" that, without ever seeing it happen, I had stored these words in the realm of the fictitious. The fictitious part ended when I started writing with you while I was in search of the "ark" that would provide African American males with safe passage through a hostile sea of race- and gender-based societal problems. During this writing process led by you, I remembered that our African ancestors had the healing power that came when they drummed, slaves sang work songs to endure their drudgery, and the blues emerged as a panacea for broken hearts. Most importantly, by working through your poems, I discovered the generative power that results when we fish.

One particular poem continues to be of special significance for me, i.e., "First Steps." Each time that I read it, I think of the rope as an umbilical cord through which life-sustaining material flows. I think of the attachment, bonding, and mutual love that evolved during the years that we were connected by the rope when we fished. This is the same sustenance needed by so many young, African American, fatherless men caught up in feelings of abandonment, the tentacles of racism, and the consequences of poverty. Shielding themselves from their pain and trying to convince others that they're okay, they don the persona of being "hard," impervious to external dangers and internal conflicts. If I could give them a balm to heal their wounds, a salve to soothe their souls, then I would give them the mutual love that we have experienced. Mutual love would strengthen them through its empowering effects. It would give them attachments not only for safety's sake, but also generate a sense of self-worth and the comfort of knowing that they are capable of loving and being loved.

I don't know why so much Biblical content is running though my mind while writing this letter, but I just thought of the statement, "And now these three remain: faith, hope and love. But the greatest of these is love." I once heard my mother say, "Love will cure what money can't." The first time that I can recall hearing this was the day that I complained about the third day in a row of having a main course meal of corn from Daddy's garden and dessert from a jar of Mama's canned peaches. I said, "Corn and peaches again!" Mama quietly told me, "Just eat what I put before you. We might not have the money to buy groceries from the store, but your Daddy and I love you and love will cure what money can't."

"When the storms of life are raging," as they surely will throughout Javon's life and the lives of other African American youth, your son and all the others will need love to help them find their way. For example, the day will come when Javon learns the terrible lesson that, for some, his race and gender count not as two things in his favor but as three strikes against him. Then, because of what your love will have done for him, he will wade through that quagmire as easily as you made your way across the river last week. So, fish often with him. He just might return the love by writing with you one day.

Love,
The Bassman